THE MIND OF AN ENTREPRENEUR

MENTAL STRATEGIES FOR NAVIGATING THE
WORLD OF BUSINESS

WENDY MUHAMMAD

www.MOEToday.com

Cover and book interior designed by JuLee Brand for Kevin Anderson & Associates.

Photography by: TTChristian Photography

The Mind of an Entrepreneur / Wendy Muhammad —1st ed.

ISBN 978-1722123574

CONTENTS

W ith the rise of technology over the last two decades, life moves faster than ever. The rate of change has also accelerated. Now, imagining the digital cameras we all had only a few years ago is laughable when our phones are also our cameras, our computers, and our organizers.

Many people worry that these changes are fraying the moral fiber of our country—with all the immediacy that we have come to expect, knee-jerk reactions seem to have replaced thoughtful responses. But that complaint really captures the heart of the problem. Morality hasn't declined; our collective consciousness has failed to keep up with the increased pace of change.

One of the main areas where rapid changes are reshaping the game is work. Keeping your head down, doing your job, and trusting that everything will work out simply doesn't work anymore. Yet personal accountability is more critical today than ever before. There is no longer anywhere to hide that isn't vulnerable to exposure. There are surveillance cameras on every corner, in every establishment, and on every block—including traffic cameras that mail you a ticket when your conduct on the road is other that what it should be. This means we have to either become more mindful of our conduct and behavior, or deal with the consequences of our poor decisions.

In addition, we have access to more tools that help us get all up in each other's business. Personal privacy has become one of the hot button issues of the day, with barely a month going by without the revelation of yet another data breach even among some of the world's most prestigious companies or organizations. We all have to come to terms with mistakes and mishaps much more quickly. The ways we handled mistakes in days past no longer work.

All these changes mean self-improvement and adaptability are more critical than ever. When all we had to do to survive was to follow the rules of employment, we didn't have to worry about improving ourselves or elevating our consciousness in order to maintain a living. We reserved that for church on the weekends and made money based on how well we performed at work. While we may have focused on becoming more productive, this mindset didn't force us to be better people. As a result, the level of universal unconsciousness has risen.

What we became instead of better people was better consumers—of material goods, cars, homes, clothing, entertainment, you name it. But we also became more voracious consumers. As more and more employees began to enjoy increased spending power, they demanded even more spending power so that they could consume more. During the boom times before the recession, employee wages increased and more businesses formed to provide the products and services the working class was clamoring for.

The escalation in compensation and consumption created a silent bubble that has now burst. Free or cheap labor is a thing of the past and companies now feel the crunch. Mergers, acquisitions, buyouts, and other corporate tools are now necessary to maintain revenue flow. For employees, this has meant layoffs, stagnant or reduced wages, fewer benefits, terminations, lost pensions, and decreased access to disability coverage and family leave.

Our fate isn't as dire as these facts may suggest it is. The changing world isn't something to be afraid of or to bemoan; it's a moral call to action. The bursting of the bubble is merely the universe's way of shaking things up and creating a rise in our consciousness. Remember the old saying, "What goes on in the dark always comes to light?" Well, today, the light has been flipped on.

ENTREPRENEURSHIP CAN USHER IN A NEW AGE OF CIVILIZATION

As the economy continues to correct itself and the universe keeps on shaking things up, many are turning to entrepreneurship as a way to sustain themselves, either by choice or, more commonly, because they have no choice. In today's world, more of us must do for ourselves or die. And many will prolong their suffering before they accept that the old business models no longer work. They simply will not be able to find a job. And if they do find a job, it will not compensate what they think they should earn or even what they need to earn in order to maintain the lifestyle they desire. For some, the changing reality of work will break their bank account. For others, it will break their hearts.

But for every old opportunity that no longer exists, there are three more that have far greater potential—for true prosperity, character development, and contribution to the world—than any job that requires you to punch the clock while looking over your shoulder.

We are living in exciting times. We have more millionaires today than ever before and so-called minorities or marginalized people are attracting wealth in record numbers. It is a great time to be an entrepreneur.

As a true entrepreneur, your performance, and the energy you bring to it, determines not just whether you are successful or not—it also determines whether you eat or have a roof over your head. Unlike with a 9-to-5 job—where you may rely on a check coming in every two weeks—if you are an entrepreneur and you don't conduct yourself properly in a meeting with a potential client, for example, you may not be able to pay your rent. That reality triggers a whole new set of emotions that you have to manage.

This hard reality is actually a blessing. It requires you to evolve your consciousness and move up into a higher vibrational energy. When you have to attract customers in order to eat, you will have no choice but to transform into the person who can stay steady in the face of fear. You will work to get into mental and emotional shape if it means that you will starve if you don't. You will learn to become resilient and to problem-solve without panicking. You will do it because you have no choice. And you will be so glad you did. Because there is no feeling better than knowing that you have provided for yourself. It is empowering. It also changes the world for the better.

The growth process that entrepreneurship requires helps to create standards and codes of conduct in the community and the world at large. Your heightened level of consciousness contributes to the establishment of a more civilized world. Your self-improvement process will contribute to community development and global moral evolution. The sooner you accept and embrace the reality, the sooner it will become true.

If you are thinking of opening a business—and because you are holding this book, you clearly are, unless you have already opened a business—it's time to acknowledge and accept that you need to undergo mental, emotional, and even physical training in order to be successful.

Entrepreneurial skills are more valuable than money, and just as important as ideas. Best-selling author and business school professor Dr. Dennis Kimbro says that the average person has more than one idea in their lifetime that could create a major transformation. The question is, what do you do with your ideas? Do you launch them into the world? Or do you talk about them around the dinner table and then fail to create a plan of action?

The missing piece for so many people with a desire—or a need—to create their own financial success is the mindset needed to start, maintain, endure, and triumph as entrepreneurs. In order to develop this mindset, you need to learn from someone who has been there.

WHO AM I TO GUIDE YOU?

As a little girl, I dreamed of owning a hotel, an NBA team, and a hospital—just for starters! I had a great childhood with parents who worked very hard to maintain our middle-class lifestyle. They pushed us to work hard and to be ourselves. I cared more about learning and studying business than I did about going outside to play. My mom used to bring home the Kiplinger Business Report and I would stay up late reading each new edition over and over. I put them all in a notebook after I read them and pretended to be a businesswoman.

Once I was grown, I was blessed to embark on a corporate career as an auditor. Since striking out on my own I have been a business consultant, developer, and crisis manager. All these roles allowed me to learn about and understand hundreds of business models and industries.

While I was a rock star in the corporate world, when I finally set out as an entrepreneur I felt like a fish out of water. I doubted my abilities left and right. I was a hard worker. I was smart. I had business experience but struggled to make the transition from technician, per se, to entrepreneur. I had all the right professional components, but needed to tweak my mental strategies in order to make the money that I felt validated my commitment and allowed me the freedom to create for a living.

After years of study, prayer, discipline, and mental, emotional, physical, and spiritual training, I realized that I didn't have the mind of an entrepreneur. My heart was too soft. I thought everyone wanted me to have what I wanted, and that I just had to show up and the world would hand me my rewards. I allowed myself to get bumped around, bruised, hit in the head, talked about, neglected, and pretty much left for dead all because I thought being smart and having a good work ethic was enough.

I made an unconscious decision to fight through to the next level, and then the next level. I fought and fought, changing, improving, tweaking, learning, and evolving. I kept climbing and learning and picking up the skills needed to develop the mind of an entrepreneur that so greatly serves me today.

During my entrepreneurial career, I have developed and managed over $200 million in businesses and projects. This has given me unique technical, emotional, strategic, risk, political, spiritual, financial, and interpersonal experiences that I couldn't duplicate if I tried. I have insight on a variety of industries, including nonprofit, religious, entertainment, insurance, banking, real estate, manufacturing, energy, and financial services. And now, I want to share some of what I learned to help you transform the energy that is currently imprisoning you.

Before I published this book, I wanted to ensure that I had been able to personally earn a minimum of a million dollars. So, if you are reading this book that means that I've done that and then some.

I wrote this book not as a technical manual: I'm not going to talk about how to write a business plan, apply for a business license, or obtain venture capital. (If you are interested in that you can hire me as a business developer and I will be delighted to help you.) I wrote this book to open you up to the transformation that must take place in your mind in order to free yourself from the failing business models and economic infrastructures that you are currently dependent upon.

It's about raising your consciousness or vision so that you can succeed as an entrepreneur. It's about closing the gap between where you are now and where you want to be. It's about learning to become the person you need to be in order to attract what you want. Because the future belongs to those who prepare for it today.

Are you ready to create a mind without borders and the financial success that only you are capable of creating?

CHAPTER 1

MARGINALIZATION IS AN EQUAL OPPORTUNITY OFFENDER

"If opportunity doesn't knock, build a door." — *Milton Berle*

If you are part of any marginalized community, whether because of your race, gender, economic class, health, age, family status, or life circumstances, jobs are scarce. Marginalization is a term that has been used mostly to refer to low-income, urban, and minority communities that have lacked or been denied access to the social and economic opportunities that the broader society enjoys. So many of us who do not fit that exact description may not consider ourselves marginalized. But the real truth is that we are all marginalized in some way.

Whether you are a 70-year-old retiree, a disabled veteran, a returning citizen, or a stay-at-home mom trying to reenter the workforce, you are marginalized. But these are just the most obvious examples—marginalization casts a much wider net. Even today's college graduates are marginalized (by prospective employers) in the pursuit of limited opportunities for highly specialized jobs; soldiers returning from overseas deployments face marginalization as people who have been "out of the workforce" despite the important jobs they did in the military; women and minorities continue to be marginalized with respect to equal pay and career advancement; people who have faced legal hardships, whether financial ones like home foreclosures, or even previous criminal issues are marginalized. It is all too likely that you will at some point find yourself on the fringe of society and denied opportunities, whether economic, social, or career-oriented ones.

If you have been underserved, disregarded, ostracized, harassed, persecuted or sidelined, you can be considered marginalized. Additionally if you have been stereotyped by society or typecast by your employer into a dead-end job (a common tactic to induce higher paid employees to leave), you can be considered marginalized.

There is good news here, though, for those willing to let it in: Entrepreneurship—whether you start a full-fledged business or become an independent contractor—is the way out of poverty, frustration, fear, and unemployment for marginalized people around the world.

> **"** Entrepreneurship—whether you start a full-fledged business or become an independent contractor—is the way out of poverty, frustration, fear, and unemployment for marginalized people around the world. **"**

Whether you want to work for yourself or not; whether you think you can be independent or can not; it doesn't really matter anymore. Entrepreneurship is truly the only viable choice to the majority of us, whether we can be considered marginalized by any definition of the word or not. If you don't seek to forge your own path, you will soon find yourself either in poverty or in a vicious cycle of being limited only to what someone else can give you, begging for and complaining about jobs that simply don't exist, are not available to you, or that pay much less than you are worth. If you are reading this, you are likely already consumed by this cycle of gloom and doom.

The way out is to change your mindset, stop waiting for a job to solve all your problems, and get up and do something for yourself.

THE PRESENT REALITY AND FUTURE OF WORK

Most of us recognize that the days of choosing a lifetime profession, getting a job, and working for one company for your entire career are long gone. But you may not realize exactly how dramatically that stereotypical reality has changed: The U.S. Bureau of Labor Statistics (BLS) reported in September 2016 that the median number of years that wage and salary workers stay with their current employers continues to decline, dropping to 4.2 years as of January of that year. Yet if you talk to salaried workers in the street, even that figure seems exceedingly high. A recent survey conducted by Randstad, a global HR services company, found that, "More than half of global human capital leaders expect to transfer one-third of their permanent positions to contingent roles in the near future." In other words, a continuing trend of diminishing long-term, full-time jobs in favor of lower paying part-time and temporary positions without essential benefits like healthcare.

Technology has expedited change at an exponential rate and the business world is changing so rapidly that many can barely keep up. College degrees are no longer a guarantee of a good job, this despite the astronomically rising cost of a college education. Neither is physical skill or manual craftsmanship. Robotics and automation technology are rapidly taking over manufacturing jobs; they also increasingly threaten many service jobs. The website Futurism reports that: "After a Chinese factory replaced 90% of its human workforce with automated machines, it experienced a 250% increase in productivity and an 80% drop in defects...as technology improves, the range of tasks that can be taken over by automated systems will continue to expand, leaving the future of human labor in a state of flux."

If you are waiting for your old manufacturing jobs to come back, or praying for politicians to change trade policies that will keep big companies here, let's face it, it's not going to happen. There is no going back to the past. Even the manufacturing jobs that do remain are increasingly being performed by robots operating in ultra-modern state-of-the-art factories. The same is true of many service jobs, such as human customer service representatives being replaced by online do-it-yourself ordering and fulfillment computer software. Every grocery store now has self-checkout lines, and in January of 2018, Amazon opened its first completely checkout-free grocery store in Seattle, where items chosen by shoppers are automatically tabulated and billed through their smartphones. In fact, many front-line service jobs are morphing into entrepreneurial pursuits, such that taxi and limousine fleet companies are giving way to independent Uber drivers, or the way that Airbnb is competing with the traditional hospitality industry. (Uber-style business models are currently emerging in numerous other, diverse industries.)

Entrepreneurship is the one true piece of good news to emerge from this changing landscape. The most recent survey conducted by Edelman Intelligence and jointly commissioned by the Freelancers Union and the jobsite Upwork projects that if present trends continue, a majority of U.S. workers will be independent freelancers (entrepreneurs) by the year 2027. The survey found that already, America's 57.3 million freelancers contribute $1.4 trillion to the economy. Not only are the opportunities there, they are increasingly plentiful. According to the same survey, the vast majority of freelancers believe that having a diversified portfolio of clients is significantly more secure than relying on one employer (63% agree, up 10 points since 2016). Accordingly, the survey found that the average freelancer services 4.5 clients per month.

For everyone in the workforce, education, hustle, drive, and strategic thinking are more important drivers of success than ever. The only catch is, if you want to make money and thrive in this fast-paced world of work and business, you have to have your mind right. You have to be all in.

> **If you want to make money and thrive in this fast-paced world of work and business, you have to have your mind right. You have to be all in.**

I see this as opportunity for marginalized people around the world because the playing field has begun to level. You don't have to be afraid of or intimidated by the workforce changes that are rampant throughout traditional business and industry today. You have such a more appealing, and realistic, alternative—to be truly enthusiastic and passionate about your entrepreneurial career path and the new opportunities that it offers. According to the most recent CareerBuilder survey, 22% of workers said they were planning to change jobs in 2017, possibly reflecting a high percentage of job dissatisfaction. The numbers were even higher among younger workers, as more than a third of workers aged 18 to 34 (35%) expected to change jobs in 2017. A Freelancers Union/Upwork survey also found that 54% of the U.S. workforce is not very confident that the work they do today is likely to exist in 20 years.

If you are stuck in a dead-end position, or even fearful of losing a good one because corporations are less vested in their employees than ever before, isn't the thought of charting your own enterprise exhilarating? This book is about helping you get on board with entrepreneurship with your whole self. Because you're going to need it.

What you don't need is a fancy degree or even a head for numbers in order to be a successful entrepreneur. You simply have to be about that life of thinking, creating, learning, and changing. It sounds like a cliché but it's not. Entrepreneurship is more than a path to your financial stability and success. It also requires you to discover and develop your authentic self, which then puts you on an accelerated success path on a professional and a personal level. It's a powerful upward spiral that is dynamic and stimulating. No more going to some boring desk and toiling over the same office drudgery every day, stagnating in your skills and interests. Entrepreneurship requires you to develop on every level—your skills, yes, but also your emotional intelligence. And as you grow, so do your opportunities and your bottom line.

WHERE THE GIFTS OF MARGINALIZATION CAN LEAD

As ironic as it may sound, I am one of the fortunate ones who has been marginalized my entire life. I wore thick glasses from the age of 5, which marginalized me from all the other kindergartners. As I got older, I was the only African American in the gifted math and science classes, on the cheerleading team, and in the engineering summer program. Even as a college student I was separated from the other minority students who attracted more financial and educational support from programs earmarked for minorities—I wasn't as in need of academic or financial support and so I was marginalized from the very group that was supposed to be "my people."

As an adult, my mindset, interests, religion, and diverse group of friends have marginalized me from members of my family. Those were profound proactive choices that I made, but they also positively shaped my outlook on life and my approach to business. It has made me more passionate and more embracing of those from other cultures, races, and backgrounds. I would not be a successful entrepreneur and a thought leader if I had never been marginalized and more importantly, if I did not accept the gift of marginalization. It allows me to seek diversity in the workplace and understand how it mirrors the real world. I've embraced the gift of marginalization, and have used it to fuel and shape a mind without borders.

Even as an employee—my first job was as an auditor for PricewaterhouseCoopers—I always saw myself as an entrepreneur. I ran my life like a business. I thought of myself and the services I performed at work as my own corporate entity and my paycheck was my revenue stream—and if you have a job, so should you. Just that small tweak in mindset will help you to improve your performance, take responsibility for yourself and your productivity, and prepare you for layoffs and corporate changes.

Throughout my career, I have been a real estate agent, a talent manager and producer for the entertainment industry, and a franchisee partner (of a new million-dollar Massage Envy Spa in downtown Silver Spring, Maryland). As a business consultant, I have overseen $200 million in projects for clients including the Department of the Treasury, the City of Chicago, Berkshire Hathaway, and Atlantic Records. Currently, I am the president, director of business affairs, and minority partner for the Minimally Invasive Vascular Center—a 27,000-square-foot micro-hospital for outpatient minimally invasive vascular and weight loss procedures in the metropolitan Washington, D.C., area. As a business owner and employer of over 100 people, I prefer entrepreneurial-minded employees who are willing to take ownership in a project or are excited to help build a company. These are the entrepreneurs and emerging leaders of the future and that is the caliber of people I want on my teams.

It's not about whether or not you have what it takes to be an entrepreneur. You may not have a choice. But one of the most beautiful things about entrepreneurship is that it is available to everyone. It is estimated that since 2014, the freelance workforce has been growing three times faster than the U.S. workforce overall, and 59% of freelancers report that they just started within the last three years. Furthermore, entrepreneurship can provide the combination of stability and flexibility that the 9-to-5 world so often can't. While many people think that freelancing and entrepreneurship are two different animals, the fact of the matter is that freelancing can be the bridge to a traditional business or it can simply be a way to gain access to additional income streams. Either way, in my opinion, many of the same mental strategies apply. And the plain fact of the matter is that you can do this.

The biggest barrier to becoming a successful entrepreneur is often in our own minds. We're too busy waiting for a job to save us. We resist taking responsibility for our own path. We stay stuck in old patterns of thinking that keep us from embracing a new reality. Being your own boss and becoming master of your own success requires you to think differently about what's possible, to write your own rule book, and to not get derailed by your emotions or your fears.

The Mind of an Entrepreneur is a practical guidebook to re-shaping your thoughts, beliefs, and actions so that you not only think like an entrepreneur, you know how to master the inner game that leads to success. By following the strategies outlined here, you'll learn how to free your creative mind, access your professional intuition, upgrade your relationship with money, and learn how to handle obstacles with proactive resilience and power.

There is a form of entrepreneurship that is available for everyone. You can't learn it from a textbook or a degree program. You can only learn by doing. You have to start by getting up and doing something for yourself. I have accomplished a lot and failed a lot more; I will show you in this book the things they leave out of the textbooks.

The game has changed. You can either let go of the old world, tweak your game or get dragged along—or even passed over altogether—by a fast-paced world of work that no longer offers a lifeline out of poverty. The choice is yours.

If you choose to create your own success, let's get started.

CHAPTER 2

CONVERSATIONS WITH YOURSELF: CREATE THE INNER VOICE OF AN ENTREPRENEUR

"Whether you think you can or you can't, you're right." — *Henry Ford*

The thought of having a conversation with yourself may seem quite abstract and maybe even a little crazy. But take a moment to think about how often you talk to yourself—you may not realize it, but it happens constantly, even if only subconsciously in some cases.

With every decision you have made, there was a conversation that took place in your head before you made the decision. Learning to talk to yourself in a more productive way can not only help you to improve your perception and come up with more options but it can also help you to face the facts of a situation—the foundation of great decision-making.

As an entrepreneur, I always ask myself critical questions before I make a decision. Whether I know the answer or not is irrelevant. My questions help spur an inner dialogue that forms the foundation for my decision-making process. I sit with the problem and write down questions that need to be answered. I don't try to answer them initially.

I recently gave one of my employees an assignment. But two weeks went by and I hadn't heard anything from this employee. When we finally sat down and started to discuss what happened and why, I asked, "What conversation did you have in your head about this assignment? When you recalled my instruction to call me if you had any questions, what did you say? Did you say, 'Nah I don't want to call her?' Did you say, 'I can do this on my own?' What did you say?"

I wanted the employee to understand how a different internal dialogue could have led to the project being completed, saving time and money, and avoiding an uncomfortable conversation.

In this case, asking the right internal questions would have led to the employee talking to me about the assignment. Perhaps we would have tweaked the strategy. We definitely could have saved money and time and I would not have had to pay someone who was not progressing with a project. The employee could have demonstrated an ability to think critically, which would have earned my trust and more future assignments.

How often do you waste time with demeaning self-talk that inhibits your ability to find a solution or, better yet, ask a question?

Controlling your self-talk is critical to your success as an entrepreneur. It can help you to explore options that can lead to better solutions. It can help you overcome fears and give you courage. It can be used to develop nuanced plans. Conversely, failure to control your inner self-talk can have the opposite effect.

For example, I have been in situations where I was trying to solve a big problem, where there was a strict deadline involved, but I spent more time inner dialoguing about what I thought the others involved in the project were thinking and trying to protect my image while consequently upping my stress levels. This conflictive form of my inner dialogue generated physical reactions including headaches, for example. Yet, once I settled down and changed the conversation I was having with myself, I realized that the solution was right in front of my face. As my grandmother used to say, "If it was a snake it would have bit me." I had had the solution all along, but I was distracted by the emotions and physical ailments caused by my inner dialogue. I wasted time and energy being worried and reacting to a story I created in my head. Had I been more mindful of my inner dialogue as soon as the problem arose, I could have saved myself a few days of agony—as well as wasteful indecision.

THE IMPORTANCE OF SELF-TALK

We are constantly talking to ourselves. This internal dialogue directly affects our emotions, which ultimately influence our decisions. And most often, this emotional effect is negative, because we tend to think negative thoughts over and over again and dwell on what we don't want. We tear ourselves down instead of telling ourselves words of encouragement and support or simply focusing on a solution or strategic approach.

Napoleon Hill, author of the classic book Think and Grow Rich, wrote, "Whatever the mind can conceive it can achieve." Everything we do begins with a thought. You are or will become what you think about most. On your road to developing the mind of an entrepreneur, learning to purposely use your thoughts and self-talk to help you strategize and sort through facts and emotions and to motivate yourself is critical to your success.

Learning how to change your mental and emotional states with inner dialogue is an invaluable tool. If you are constantly telling yourself that you don't have the money to start your business, or if you are having trouble getting started because you keep telling yourself that it won't work, then simply changing your inner dialogue can create the shift to positive thinking that you need.

Believe me, I had all the negative thoughts before I stepped out as an entrepreneur. I had to consciously decide to start thinking more supportive, strategic, and productive thoughts. I had always been a hard worker as an employee, so I started telling myself, "If I can work hard and go above and beyond expectations for someone else, I rtainly do it for myself. If I'm smart enough to figure it out for someone else, I can figure it out for myself."

Most of what we base our decisions on is the story that our thoughts are telling us, or the opinions of others, and not reality. One experience from early in my career—when I submitted one of my first proposals as a consultant—exemplifies this split between perception and reality well. As I sat in my car before I entered the building to drop off my proposal I had an inner dialogue with myself that went something like this: "They are not going to accept your proposal. They don't even work with African Americans. If you don't get this, you may as well go and find a job. You can't do this. They probably don't even respect women. And you're definitely not dressed right!" I spent 20 minutes in that car rehearsing rejection, and doing so on multiple levels! I was upset. I cried. I had a headache. And I was dwelling in the wrong mindset.

Fortunately, in this instance, I chose to take my focus away from this line of thinking, gather myself up, and walk inside the building to attend the meeting where I would make my case. They accepted me for the project and became my consulting client—all that self-punishment had been a total lie! It had also been a waste of valuable psychological energy.

There were other instances when my negative self-talk prevented me from even writing a proposal or making a phone call. I was hindered by this more times than I care to admit. Now supportive inner dialogue or positive self-talk is an important part of my mental wellness. I never hesitate to stop and assess my thoughts and emotions, even during the busiest work days. Learning to redirect my internal dialogue has helped me to manage fears and focus on what is real. The sooner you do it too, the sooner you'll start experiencing entrepreneurial success.

UPGRADING YOUR INNER VOICE

Your inner voice has a dual nature: It is your conscience—that still small voice that speaks your wisdom and your moral code; some, in-

cluding me, think of it as the God within. But it is also you
monologue, your verbal stream of consciousness. In both
inside of you and, of course, not audible to the people around you.
(If you are having audible conversations with yourself, you may have
some other issues that you may want to address!) Because it is hidden
from view and occurs only within your own mind, it is difficult to
have much objectivity on your inner voice. So generally the first step
in improving the quality of your thoughts is to raise your awareness
of those thoughts in the first place.

Even as you are reading this book, you are having a conversation
with yourself. Perhaps you are having thoughts about this book, or
about what you want to eat for dinner, or about what happened at
work today. Or maybe you are wondering what to have for lunch or
what the weather will be tomorrow. Those conversations affect how
you internalize what you are reading, just as they affect your interpretations or what is going on around you when you are going about
every moment of your life.

If you hit your snooze button this morning, you had a dialogue
with yourself. Maybe you said, "I'm going to get up in five minutes," or
perhaps you said, "I'm not getting up" or "So what if I'm late, I'm tired."
Then, let's say you hit the snooze button five more times. In order to
finally motivate yourself to get on up, you had to change your dialogue. Perhaps you said, "Damn I'm late!" Or, "If I get up now, I'll have
time to meditate today and drink my protein shake." No matter what
you decided to do after you got up, you had some type of conversation
with yourself, either consciously or subconsciously.

If you have an argument with someone, you are likely reanalyz-
ing that argument and the corresponding emotions in your mind, via
your inner voice, long after the disagreement ends, and regardless of
the outcome. If someone does something that you don't agree with,
you'll often find yourself talking about their decision silently in your
head long after the person has walked away. Your inner voice dictates
what thoughts you hold on to, whether they are good or bad, and importantly, whether they move you forward or not.

Even though you may not be fully aware of it, your inner dialogue influences every aspect of your life. It shapes who you are, affects your decisions, and even alters your internal vibration, which can lead to either disease or a peak state of healthy well-being. As an entrepreneur, it can guarantee your success or failure—it all depends on how you use it. The good news is that you can train it to create success. If you never make the effort to train it, chances are your stream of thought will wander aimlessly without direction. You must learn to use your inner voice to help you accomplish your goals and not burden you with thoughts that are unproductive or that lead to unwanted results.

To start to understand what your inner voice is continually telling you, answer these few simple questions:

- What are some typical conversations you have with yourself?
- What do you say to yourself about yourself?
- What do you say to yourself about your business or your ideas?
- What do you say to yourself about what you want?
- And what do you say to yourself about the good that is showing up in your life?
- When something doesn't work out?
- How careful are you about the thoughts you let in to your head? Do you seek out inspiring or informative content, whether from other people, podcasts, books, magazines, or TV shows? Or do you spend most of your time doing the equivalent of reading a tabloid or gossiping around the water cooler?

"

Don't let the noise of others' opinions drown out your own inner voice. – Steve Jobs

"

THE INNER VOICE OF AN ENTREPRENEUR

A successful entrepreneur uses his or her inner voice to construct strategy, alter emotional states, motivate, and contemplate. An entrepreneur should be careful not to use her inner voice to regurgitate negativity, tear herself down, or promote adverse behaviors.

This same discretion must be used for the voices of other people that you let in to your own head. As an entrepreneur you must be mindful of naysayers. Outside influences can become part of the fabric of your subconscious mind very rapidly. For example, if you hear a song on the radio on your way to work or school in the morning, how many times do you notice that song running through your head all day long, even if you don't even like the song? That is how spongy your mind is. For that reason, you must guard against covert negativity and being influenced by individual and collective mindsets that are stagnant, unproductive, and destructive.

There may be times when friends and family members do not share your vision. Often in their desire to protect you they will discourage you and work to influence your decisions in ways that are detrimental to your personal and professional growth. They will sometimes create conditions and emotional scenarios themed with their limited beliefs. Before you know it, you've subconsciously adopted fears and begun to produce conditions that did not originate with you. Beware! These conditions can create an unproductive inner dialogue and can ultimately affect your choices in negative ways.

Your subconscious mind is your connection to the universe and its endless supply of ideas and inspirations. Your inner mental environment must be protected. When carefully cultivated, a vibrant, steadfast, positive, and flexible subconscious mind gives birth to life-changing conditions. But once it becomes imprisoned by fears and negativity it will produce conditions that reflect and perpetuate those emotions.

CULTIVATING THE MENTAL FLEXIBILITY TO FACE ANY OBSTACLE

An evolved entrepreneur understands that the condition of his business is a result of the thoughts and conversations he has with himself. An entrepreneur filled with negative, limited self-talk will have a weak spirit, will be slow to action, will produce minimal results, and will have lackluster financial success.

Your inner voice must drive you to action. Einstein observed that nothing happens until something moves. Nothing that you want in business will happen until you take action. The quality of your actions will be based on the fertility of your subconscious mind.

Your inner voice functions like a muscle. I like to call it subconscious muscle. Just the way that your physical muscles have muscle memory, your subconscious mind has muscle memory as well. This muscle needs to be exercised, strengthened, and stretched in order to function in a productive manner. You must train it to serve you and support your endeavors. It is the life force through which you will create the conditions that allow you to walk with meaningful purpose.

In order to propel yourself into action, you must protect your thoughts and environment just as you would protect your newborn baby. Negativity can influence your inner voice and infect your subconscious mind like a cancer. Unsolicited negativity will undoubtedly come your way. You must masterfully translate any negativity into either motivation, an opportunity, or a lesson.

How do you do that, exactly? Look for the good in every situation. Find a way to be grateful for everything that happens—the missteps as well as the triumphs. This will help you to retrain your inner voice, reprogram your subconscious mind, and have productive conversations with yourself.

If you know in advance that you are going to be exposed to negativity, take a moment to get your thoughts straight in advance. When I know that I am going to be around negative people or people who don't value me, I make sure that my internal dialogue is right. There is also the often repeated adage that, if you start telling other people that things in your business or your life are not going well, or even simply that you are having a bad day, 80% of people don't care and the other 20% are actually happy to hear it! The sales trainer Tom Hopkins used to tell his audiences, "When people ask you how things are going in your life, you should say to them 'Unbelievable!' because that covers it either way!" By doing that, you can stop negativity in its tracks.

And like former First Lady Michelle Obama once stated, when they go low, I go high. So, I tell myself that their negativity has nothing to do with me or what I showed up on the planet to do; my purpose is bigger than they can imagine. I review my strategy and make sure my plan of action is solid and that I am comfortable with my direction. I remind myself to focus on being the best that I can be. I think of what I am grateful for. I arm myself with thoughts that prevent me from joining in on the negativity or being affected by a mindset that does not reflect my goals. Because I'm a spiritual person my affirmations and dialogue follow that track, but you should develop and use whatever sayings and affirmations resonate enough with you that they motivate you to stay true to your intentions and take actions toward your goals.

DEVELOPING PROFESSIONAL CONFIDENCE

In order to develop the inner knowing that you can be successful as an entrepreneur, you must first start by studying your craft. Know your business. Know your industry. I will walk you through how to do this very process in Chapter 4, but I'm bringing it up now because study is a powerful way to upgrade the level of your thoughts; it will help you to create strategies that will give you confidence in the face of adversity.

Your studies will also help you develop what I call professional intuition—a subconscious muscle that reacts in an industry-specific manner that serves your business. Once you have built this professional intuition, you can hone it and access it by meditating and getting quiet. Learn to sit in silence. I advise that you take time out several times throughout the day to just be silent. When a problem pops up, get quiet. When you witness a blessing, get quiet. When a major change is required, or you need to shift gears or simply write a letter, get quiet. Recognize that there is a power bigger than you. Express your gratitude to that power. Acknowledge that power. Let the energy of that power flow through you. Think positively and creatively about your business and your employees and the ways that you may be able to help both to succeed. Focus on what you want. Surround yourself with music, notes, motivation, people, and images that reflect of what you want.

When you experience something that you don't want, take a moment to focus on what you do want and be grateful that this out-of-alignment experience has put you one thought closer to your goal. Don't spend excessive amounts of time rehashing the negative situation. And whatever you do, avoid pity parties at all cost. When you notice that you have started feeling sorry for yourself, validate the facts, find something to be grateful for. Then check in with your own gut. In these ways, you do your due diligence, which will help you to move with confidence and to correct or fine-tune any existing issues. When you are marginalized or have lived your entire life in a marginalized state, it is inevitable that you will have moments when you feel defeated or where you may be insulted or doubted by others. The key is to know how to bring yourself back to that productive state. I'm very careful about watching news programs, for example, that show constant negative images of people who look like me. I'm careful to not allow these images to creep into my subconscious. If I have a big goal, I break it down into smaller, more attainable goals. This helps to build my confidence. I take it a step at a time. I use every knock as a boost and a way to gain unique knowledge and experience that I incorporate into my life strategy.

We are what our thoughts have made us; so, take care about what you think. Starting with your inner voice helps you build your business on bedrock instead of quicksand.

In the next chapter, you'll learn how to keep opening your mind and your sense of what's possible by challenging your assumptions and learning how to cultivate a mind without borders, as well as how to develop the patience and the resilience to stay on your path to entrepreneurial success.

CHAPTER 3

EXPANDED POSSIBILITIES: CULTIVATE A MIND WITHOUT BORDERS

"Thinking outside of the box keeps you from suffocating inside of one."
—Matshona Dhliwayo

We spend most of our mental energy trying to either fit in a box or get out of a box. Sometimes this is a protective box created by those who wish to keep us safe. Other times it's a set of controlling guidelines designed to direct our thinking and behaviors as marginalized people. Still other times it's social norms that are often steeped in religious, ethnic, or even corporate culture. Identifying the boxes that restrict you is critical to your development as an entrepreneur.

The "box" is the way you've been taught to look at things, do things, and all the run-of-the-mill assumptions that almost everyone else is making. We have been taught and trained all our lives on how to live and dwell in these mental, economic, and social boxes.

Most of our responses to events and people are based on whether our behavior or choices fit in the box that we have been expected to dwell in. Whether it's our parents who expect us to be married with children by a certain age or a society that says that if we are good in math or science we must be an engineer or a doctor, much of our daily stress involves either struggling to fit in a box, fighting to get out of one, or being angry because we are trapped in the virtual box. Even once we break the general barriers placed on us by our inner circle, the labels and limitations we face as society attempts to keep us marginalized are ongoing sticking points of resistance or outright agitation.

Growing up, I always wanted to be a businessperson—a mogul, as my Dad called it one day during a conversation. The concept of being a businesswoman never crossed my mind; it was always businessperson. As I matriculated through school, I consistently demonstrated a good grasp of math and science, which led one of my high school teachers to suggest that I become a family medical practitioner, psychiatrist, or an engineer. That suggestion took on a life of its own as I became aware of how excited this idea made everyone around me, including my teachers. Nothing about any of those fields of study intrigued me the way business and entrepreneurship did, but I went along because not only did I feel like it was the right thing to do (or was made unconsciously to feel that way), but I confess I truly enjoyed the feeling that I got when I watched everyone's reaction of excitement to the idea. But I must stress, it was everyone else's excitement.

I spent my first year and a half of college trying to force myself to get excited about engineering or psychiatry. When I finally gained the courage to step outside the box and focus on my first love, which was business, my whole world changed. I distinctly remember that the breeze on my face felt like prosperity as I walked on campus after making that decision. To this day, when I feel a breeze on my face, I think about that moment of liberation. I had never felt so open. At precisely that point, I felt free to see myself as a businessperson and allow my mind to explore possibilities that I had suppressed. I saw international business as I walked past the foreign cultures department. I thought about purchasing real estate and restaurant development as I sat in the cafeteria.

As a child I had pretended that when I went to school I was going to my office. I got a cash register and play money for Christmas while in grammar school and my brother and I used to play "cash register" where I was the business owner and he was the consumer. My parents even gave me a word processing typewriter that had an electronic screen on it when I was in middle school; I started doing my homework on it and pretended to be a businesswoman.

I remember the exhilaration of those creative experiences sparked by those gifts and now I started thinking like that again. I even ditched my backpack for a briefcase. The freedom and creativity were flowing and I never looked back. This was the beginning of the process of developing what I call a "mind without borders."

Much to my surprise, that would not be the last time I had to defy a label or bust out of the box. I've faced people who are sexist and only think that a woman should work for someone else, or that what I have accomplished must be attributed to a husband, a boyfriend, or a sexual relationship with a man. I've dealt with people who think that black women are only good as assistants, secretaries or, at best, vice presidents of companies owned by men. Some people I have encountered have thought that someone with the last name Muhammad can't be successful in America and can't be a beautiful addition to humanity. I've dealt with family members, close friends, and men who were only happy with me if I did what they wanted me to do. The marginalization, you see, is ongoing.

It has been my creativity that has helped me to navigate my way out of the boxes that society had placed me in. For me, having a mind without borders has meant learning how to ditch the boxes and live a life in which your mind is not preoccupied with the effort of trying to manage the expectations of others and of yourself (because it can be surprising to learn how you have participated in keeping yourself in your own version of a box).

The ability to think creatively has helped me be more flexible, explore outcomes without reacting to "what-ifs," challenge assumptions, and be open to change. And it can help you do all these things too.

THE FIRST PLACE TO OPEN THE BORDERS OF YOUR MIND IS AROUND HOW YOU SEE YOURSELF

Are you refraining from being yourself because you are afraid of what others may think? Do you allow others to define and package you? Are you always trying to conform to a set of rules that are not your own? Are you constantly stressed out because you feel as if you either have no options or very few options? Are you living in the proverbial box? Is it possible that the box you are in is contrary to who you are?

The old cliché says that we can't expect new results if we keep doing the same old things. In this same vein, you can't expect to see new possibilities if you keep thinking the same old thoughts. If you see yourself in a way that is not yielding the results you are looking for, then it's critical that you change the way you see yourself.

Reacting to the opinions of others has become the underlying theme of most of our lives. We've become so conscious of what other people are thinking that our responses, choices, and conversations are all in response to our anticipation of someone else's opinion. Living like this will most certainly lead you down a path of failure and fallen dreams. This mindset weakens you, limits your vision, and sets you up to readily accept defeat.

Living your life inside the box is the result of a belief that you have no other choices. But you always have other choices. A belief is just a thought that you keep thinking. It is not necessarily the truth. To climb out of the box you have been living in, you must begin by rewiring your mind and changing the thoughts that you entertain—and the most important beliefs to examine and change revolve around how you see yourself.

RE-WIRE YOUR BELIEFS

It is very common to do what you see everyone else doing simply because you figure that if it's good enough for them, it must be good enough for you too. But you are not like anyone else. You are a manifestation of the expressive desire of your Creator. You were not created to go with the crowd. Your existence represents an opportunity to fulfill a one-of-a-kind mission. Your mixture of talents, passions, skills, and experiences cannot be duplicated. They all add up to an absolutely unique perspective, and that perspective, particularly when it is freed of any external borders, is your currency to success.

> **Whenever you need to challenge yourself to think in a more expanded way, ask yourself: What did I show up on the planet to do?**

Whenever you need to challenge yourself to think in a more expanded way, ask yourself: What did I show up on the planet to do?

Unfortunately, most of us struggle to answer this question with enough passion to believe it and enough confidence to let it guide our actions. And so we settle for being imitations of something or someone else. To harness our potential and use it to create success, we must learn to think outside the box and explore options that help us to think without the borders that society, the corporate world, and even our school systems try to impose upon us.

Whatever box you have been living inside of, it's not real. It is a construct—a set of ideas that you have thought over and over and over again until they coalesced into a hardened belief, or a system of related and equally limiting beliefs.

A belief is nothing more than a thought that you keep thinking. When those beliefs are too small or are simply wrong for you, they no longer support your goals. In fact, they are limiting; they only serve to hold you back. Some examples of limiting beliefs include: There's only so much money (or opportunity) to go around. I'm not good at numbers. I'm too stupid to figure this out. Can you see how thinking these types of thoughts over and over again will limit your possibilities and your confidence in yourself? If you want to step outside the box, your limiting beliefs have got to go.

The best way to start thinking out of the box is to first identify and challenge all the assumptions that you feel are limiting your progress or are psychologically imprisoning you. Let's start by writing down a goal. Then list all the conventionally held ideas about what the steps are to achieving that goal. Next, write down your worries and fears about completing that step—those limiting thoughts that you need to overcome. Finally, write down what you need to believe in order to take that step and find success.

Let's say, for example, that you are an artisan jewelry maker and you want to sell your unique jewelry designs in a major department store. According to the industry standard process, the steps you'll likely have to take to reach that goal include: meeting with a buyer, finding a distributor, and selling through a smaller retail outlet first, as a means of developing a previous sales history. Now write down the beliefs you have about your ability to complete each step. Remember, a belief is simply a thought that you keep thinking persistently. They can be changed. But if you don't know what belief you currently have, you won't know what thoughts you have to re-wire.

If you find yourself having limiting beliefs—such as, no buyer is going to want to take a meeting with me—as you review the list, simply ask yourself, "What other ways can I think about this?" Try making smaller milestones along the way that are more achievable. Whenever you get stuck and lose faith in yourself, ask yourself, "Why do I think this to be true? Why does this keep popping into my head?" It could be fear or a limiting belief that you adopted from someone else. Take that belief and hold it up to the light—you will see, upon closer examination, that it simply isn't true. Keep looking for alternative interpretations until you find a thought that gives you the hope you need to keep moving forward toward that goal instead of deciding it will never work and giving up.

As you are navigating through this process, accept the fact that challenging your stagnant beliefs and choosing to embrace more inspiring beliefs is not easy. If it were easy, everyone would be doing it. It is a process—it's not add water and stir. You have to educate yourself about the business processes of your industry and it is imperative that you commit to lifelong learning and put in the spiritual and intellectual labor. You must practice patience, be steadfast, develop coping skills, and have the resilience to implement what you've learned. If you expect instant success, or an infusion of cash from an angel investor, you will quit if it doesn't happen, which is a shame because the likelihood of this really happening is slim. For the vast majority of entrepreneurs, the belief that an investor will come along and save you and give you the money you need to launch your business is a limiting belief.

As I write this, I was recently in Johannesburg, South Africa, speaking to a group of entrepreneurs sponsored by a trendsetting magazine called Wealth Ladder. As I sat there listening to the other speakers and to the sideline discussions among the entrepreneurs in the room, it became clear to me that nearly everyone there thought the best way to grow their business was to find an investor. So imagine how disappointed they were when it came my turn to speak, and I began by saying that most of them would never find an investor.

This does not mean that I thought their fledgling businesses and entrepreneurial dreams were doomed. Far from it! I encouraged them to barter services and to be creative—to use whatever means were available to them, and from whatever point at which they were starting, and by doing so they would start moving forward much more authentically and quickly than spending all their time and energy looking and hoping for an investor to "save" them. They reminded me of singers in a talent show waiting to be chosen by the judges as the winner. My message was "stop waiting to get chosen and chose yourself." But I don't think that many of the people in that room heard that message because they were so disappointed by my opening statement.

However, the reality, according to Forbes, is that most start-up businesses don't qualify for venture capital and never will. The Small Business Administration estimates that of the roughly 600,000 new businesses that are launched in the United States each year, the number of start-ups funded by venture capital is only about 300. This means that the probability of an average new business getting venture capital is about 0.0005%. It also means that 99.95% of entrepreneurs will not get venture capital at start-up. Some of you are already about to put this book down and quit. But stick with me: the larger reality is that you can be successful in business if you are creative. Even if you have received venture capital funding, but your mind isn't in the right spot, your business still won't work. So you still need this book!

Whenever you see a highly successful person, chances are there are years of work, of both failure and success, that you didn't see. But you don't need an immediately thriving business in order to be considered successful. You can start from where you are with what you've got and build a bridge from there. You can begin by supplementing your current income from your job with one viable product or service and then expand. It takes some people 10 years to find the right path and develop the right mindset and then another 10 years to master their craft or service. The good news is that technology and the internet have accelerated the speed at which we can become successful in business. And with the help of the techniques in this book, it likely won't take you 10 years to get your mind right.

OUT-OF-THE-BOX THINKING CAN DISRUPT AN ENTIRE INDUSTRY

Here's an example of a box that needed to be broken out of, and a case of where it happened in a big way. In the 1970s and '80s, the music industry restricted access to artists who were pioneering hip-hop. They were shut out from distribution, mainstream radio, and television. Even ABC News has acknowledged that when hip-hop began, corporate America ignored it. Big mistake.

Hip-hop culture now generates more than $10 billion per year and has moved beyond its musical roots, transforming into a dominant and increasingly lucrative lifestyle. I am a member of the generation that contributed to changing business models in the entertainment industry. I worked with many artists and helped to organize and identify independent sales and performance outlets. We created advertising and found independent distributors and manufactured our own CDs. We created branded T-shirts and clothing and focused on lifestyle. Even today, I focus all my businesses on creating a lifestyle and branding nontraditional lifestyle items. For example, I designed a Movado watch branded with our healthcare company logo. These are all examples of thinking outside of the box with a mind without borders. These artists I worked with were marginalized and became entrepreneurs as a way out of the proverbial box that they had been relegated to. I remember how people laughed at me and thought I had gone crazy when I called myself a business developer and my clients were members of the yet-to-hit-it-big hip-hop community. I remember being ridiculed when I suggested that artists stop printing CDs and release their albums digitally, online. No one was doing that at the time. People thought I was crazy. However, it was one of the most rewarding periods in my career because I was thinking outside the box, being creative and innovative. To this day, I continue to have the utmost respect for those men and women in the underground hip-hop scene across the United States but especially in Chicago, who allowed me to witness and be a part of the concept of minds without borders. I've always hoped that my creativity enriched their lives as much as their stories motivated me.

BREAKING OUT OF YOUR OWN BOX

In order to climb your way out of the boxes that you've been existing within, you must define the existing assumptions that you habitually rely upon. I'm not talking about being deliberately weird or purposefully being contrary or difficult. I'm talking about having the courage to think for yourself, to plot your own course, and to take conventional wisdom with a grain of salt.

If you are going to live an extraordinary life you must have extraordinary thoughts and you must open yourself up to more options. If you want to do new things, you must develop new thoughts. Look at what everyone else is doing and think of something different, or even extraordinary. Employ thoughts that stretch beyond your existing belief system. Embrace your own gifts and the lessons your life story has taught you and chart a course that is uniquely your own.

Entrepreneurs are often pioneers and are not afraid to create their own belief systems or to think beyond what they were taught as children or in school. They are not afraid of being told no or even being laughed at. Thinking without borders is a part of their personal mantra and can be as obvious as creating a unique product or as complex as doing what no one else has done before. It can also be as simple as developing a product or service that solves a small problem in a big industry.

Who do you idolize? Is it a sports player, a musical artist, a businessperson, or an innovator? Study their lives and their thinking—read their biography or memoir, listen to their old interviews. You will see that they thought and acted differently than other people, and that's why they achieved such great heights.

If you want to be successful and accomplish great things and realize unbelievable dreams you must train your brain to think outside the box, consistently. You must give yourself permission to be different. Tell yourself that it's okay. When you strive to be yourself, you will attract people and circumstances that support who you are.

Would Einstein have discovered the theory of relativity if he were not thinking outside the box? Here is what Walter Isaacson, the former CEO of CNN, a professor of history at Tulane University, and the author of several biographies of some of history's most influential men, said of Einstein: "I think the great thing to realize is that Einstein wasn't, say, smarter than Max Planck or Lorenz or some of the other people at the time...but he could think more creatively. He was more willing to think out of the box, to use a cliché. To think, well, maybe we don't have to be boxed in by what Newton said about space and time. So, it wasn't that he had some unattainable intelligence. It was that he was a little bit more creative, more willing to defy convention and to think a little bit differently from everybody else."

I do have one word of warning to share: as you are moving from inside the box to outside the box you may feel alone. Just move with confidence knowing that you will attract relationships and circumstances that agree with your desires, but it may feel like you are isolating yourself at first. Know that you are not alone. When you step out beyond the borders that society, your family, and your own limited thinking have tried to keep you in, you will attract everyone and everything that you need.

> **When you step out beyond the borders that society, your family, and your own limited thinking have tried to keep you in, you will attract everyone and everything that you need.**

Thinking outside the box ignites your creative forces. It helps you to explore and figure out who you are. It allows you to approach challenges and create strategies that are fresh and that magnetize new opportunities and just the right people to you. It produces groundbreaking results that have the potential to create an avalanche of popularity and wealth. The world is starving for new ideas and authentic people. Thinking without borders is what opens all doors.

CHAPTER 4

SMART IS THE NEW RICH: LEVERAGE YOUR PERSONAL EXPERIENCES TO INCREASE YOUR KNOWLEDGE

"Ignorance is no longer an adequate excuse for failure. Why? Because virtually all limitation is self-imposed. You will soon realize that you, the individual, are a minute expression of the Creator of all things and as such, you have no limitations except those accepted in your own mind." — Dennis Kimbro

Conventional wisdom tells us to study hard, go to college, get a good job, to strive for regular job-level promotions and a path of steady (but largely predictable) career advancement. "Smart" in our society is often defined not by innate intelligence, but by how well you follow these guidelines and comply with societal norms. And so we buy into the concept that we must strive to progress from management trainee to junior and then senior management, then to the executive level, for example. But this line of escalation is not always available—particularly to anyone who has been marginalized—and, moreover, can take a significant number of years to accomplish. Even when we do manage to achieve this linear progression, we often find ourselves disappointed because we so rarely enjoy the work or find it meaningful. The disappointment is compounded when we think we've followed the rules and done everything "right."

As a little girl, I always thought that being smart would make me rich. So I studied hard and read a lot. Imagine my surprise when I grew up and realized that all smart people weren't rich! What I learned early in my career is that our society's definition of smart often makes mediocrity—in terms of income as well as overall professional and personal fulfillment—the goal.

WHAT SMART REALLY MEANS

Being smart means being able to analytically approach the constantly shifting mosaic of the modern workplace and global economy with openness. It is a commitment to continual evolution. Smart is not a stagnant concept; it represents a process that never ends. Once you graduate from college, for example, you're not done. Earning your bachelor's degree may be an important step, but it is only one accomplishment in a lifelong journey of learning.

Intelligence doesn't always come from books, either. As you embark on your entrepreneurship journey, you may be surprised to learn that you have more experience and more knowledge in more areas of life than you may think. Whatever you have accomplished in life has required some specific sets of skills. Whether you grew up in a war-torn country or in the urban neighborhoods of inner-city America, survived abuse, lived to be 75 years old, thrived through a prison sentence, or earned an honor society designation in school, each of these experiences required a set of skills that have laid the foundation for who you are. Perseverance, strategic planning, public relations, emotional intelligence, human resources are all examples of skills that you likely have used to get where you are today. A crucial piece of being smart is learning to identify those skill sets within yourself and developing them to the point that you rival that successful corporate executive or billionaire entrepreneur that you admire. But being smart is only half the battle. Taking action is where the real power is ignited.

As important as this step is, it's not enough to uncover the existing knowledge that you have cultivated throughout your lifetime as a result of your experiences—you must value this intelligence, despite the fact that you may feel marginalized. If you're 70 and can't get a job but you have a lifetime of skills and knowledge, you've got to be the one to value it and offer it to others.

Your knowledge is your currency. What you have in your mind, no one can take away from you. And it can always be increased; no matter how many important skills you already have or things you already know, you can always grow your knowledge. And in turn, you can always use your knowledge to help you grow.

> **"**
>
> **Your knowledge is your currency. What you have in your mind, no one can take away from you.**
>
> **"**

THE COST OF IGNORANCE

Have you ever been around someone who really didn't realize how uninformed they were? I've had people who work for me who have complained that they just don't know what to do or how to put the project plan together. My business partner often says, "Well you don't know what you don't know." And in order to achieve outstanding results you are only as good as what you can make happen. So being resistant to research, education, or coaching, for example, can impact your performance and ultimately your finances.

Many people may talk a good game and may even be fooling others, but they don't even have enough knowledge to know (that is, to truly understand) what they don't know. Ponder that for a minute. They sound intelligent—they use advanced language, and from their intonation and their confidence they come across as intellectual. (We see this type of person so much in pop culture and now also in political arenas.) And yet they have no idea that they are unlikely to be successful. Often, the people listening to this person are also so uninformed or ignorant that they don't recognize that the person they're listening to and regarding as knowledgeable is just regurgitating nonsense. Then those listeners go out and repeat the ignorant words and fake knowledge spreads as if it were gospel. The next thing you know, you find yourself dependent upon bogus information that makes no sense and you're wondering why you aren't making the progress toward the goals you want to achieve.

Not only do you not want to rely on this person, you don't want to be this person. You should strive to be so knowledgeable about yourself, your client, and your product or service that your professional intuition is keen and deeply developed.

As a businessperson, I've always studied and obtained additional certifications in the areas that I have worked in. I love real estate development, so I study every aspect of it—from marketing and sales to construction and regulations regarding permits and variances and the like. As a consultant, I have spent countless hours studying the respective specific industries of my clients, as well as information that applies across all industries, including organizational development, traditional business models, organizational charts, production processes; you name it. Whenever I had a commute, I took the opportunity to use that valuable time to study and learn, reading while I was commuting by train or airplane, or listening to motivational podcasts and lectures while I was driving in my car.

Why have I dedicated so much time to studying when I was already working in the industry I was learning about? Because lack of knowledge is the kiss of death for entrepreneurs. Your competitors, employees, and clients can gauge exactly where you are by how much knowledge you have. If you merely think you know what you are talking about but haven't studied, sooner or later it will show and it will hurt you.

You see this a lot in the African American community. Our business endeavors do not tend to follow our passions, authenticity, knowledge, or educational base, nor do they solve problems in our community. Rather, they are often based on what we see someone else doing; whether that's via pop culture trends or the often limited industry that is already finding success in our community.

So, for example, if we see someone making money in real estate we may decide that we're going into the field of real estate also. We may have no training other than the fact that we've purchased a house or condo in the past or we know someone that has recently purchased real estate. But the person we are trying to emulate may have a master's degree in real estate development. Or, for example, we may have a friend or relative who is doing well in a particular field and so we think that their success is due to the fact that they chose the right profession. But what we oftentimes neglect to acknowledge is that their knowledge base on the subject matter may be so deep that they make it look easy. Or that person may be taking a risk that we have not analyzed. Whatever we choose to do from a business standpoint must be accompanied by knowledge. The most successful businesses are those that solve problems, and there are plenty of problems in the African American community. We must train ourselves to focus on our authenticity and direct our creative energy toward solving problems instead of hopping on the pop culture bandwagon.

Often when we don't have enough knowledge, we tend not to respect knowledge as much as we should. We have all likely heard the stereotype that all kids in the hood want to be rappers or basketball players even if they can't rap or bounce a ball. We do the same thing as adults, when we allow our limited knowledge to prevent us from being unique and building a business or career around our individual gifts or skill sets. We often fall into this groupthink because we have no concept of individual intelligence, goals, or uniqueness, and we haven't trained ourselves how to solve problems. On top of that, we diss knowledge and try to do whatever we have seen work for someone else. Sometimes we are successful enough to get by. Other times we spend most of our time angry at the successful person because they won't help us to do exactly what they've done to get where they are. Go figure!

Another way our lack of knowledge tends to keep us marginalized is that we will choose a profession not because we saw someone else do it, but because we saw it on TV. Thousands of minority young people follow career trends that are often presented in 60-second commercials—such as programs to train medical or dental assistants, massage therapists, and auto mechanics. But in the vast majority of cases, these opportunities have no relationship to our innate intelligence or earned knowledge. It seems like a slam dunk and then when we end up not liking or doing well at the work, we further marginalize ourselves by losing hope.

This behavior is a result of our extreme desire to be successful yet ignoring, or overlooking, our innate instinct that tells us that we should be doing something for ourselves instead of trying to force ourselves into jobs and careers that don't align with our talents or desires. Consider becoming an entrepreneur. You can start off small and work at it on the side, per se, while you are in school or working a job to make ends meet.

Tweaking your mindset so that you make it your goal to discover your own personal interests and skills is a much more productive way to become an entrepreneur or to start a career than simply copying what someone else has done. Resist the urge to pursue a business or career simply because it sounds good to others—that may sound obvious, but I can't tell you how many physicians and engineers I've met who hate their work; they went into the field only because it sounded good and it garnered a fair amount of attention from their family, teachers, and peers. I understand the perception that, "I'm in medical school," gets a more positive response than, "I'm a janitor working to develop a cleaning company because I love cleanliness." Who do you think will likely be happier and more successful, the physician who hates medicine or the entrepreneurial janitor who loves building a business devoted to cleanliness? But the emotional response we get from others' reactions to our goals is often what drives us in the wrong direction. That's why knowledge that helps you to create a unique strategy that works for you will supercharge your drive, determination, and perseverance despite naysayers, haters, and those who just don't understand—people who don't have your vision.

A CLEAR DEFINITION OF KNOWLEDGE

Knowledge is generally defined as facts, information, and skills acquired by a person through experience or education; the theoretical or practical understanding of a subject; awareness or familiarity gained by experience of a fact or situation. Here's what knowledge is not: rumors, false information, assumptions, or emotional interpretations of situations.

As an entrepreneur, you must learn to take your emotions out of the equation when analyzing a situation so that you can more clearly gather the facts. Your emotions are not part of the factual content. After you gather your knowledge you can selectively entertain any emotional factors. Do not exercise poetic license when gathering and analyzing facts for your business. Train your staff to do the same. There is nothing worse than relying on a staff member to gather information and report details about an event when their emotions are running high. Learn to sift through what I call poetic licensing so that your decision is based on facts and not the colorful presentation of the person relaying the information—and that goes for you too, when you are the person gathering and presenting the facts that you'll use to make a decision.

Another habit you must break yourself of is doing things just because you see other people doing them. It is certainly acceptable to admire and be motivated by someone else and the success they have achieved in their own unique way. It also makes sense to learn from the mistakes of others and get ideas on what works and what doesn't work by examining their entrepreneurial journey. If you mimic someone, know why you are doing it. Have a purpose. But be sure to weave in your own experiences and your knowledge of the subject to solve your problems and seek creative solutions. Your goal should be to become the subject matter expert in your endeavor of choice; if you can't, hire an expert or barter with an expert. There are plenty of affordable resources out there, from business- and industry-specific seminars, to adult education courses at community colleges—even some reputable content on the internet for passionate entrepreneurs to educate themselves. Taking action based on good knowledge and facts is the most powerful way to lead your employees and yourself.

CHAPTER 5

STAY AUTHENTIC: DEVELOP YOUR PROFESSIONAL INTUITION

"Don't you dare underestimate the power of your own instinct. Instinct is a lifesaver for sharks and entrepreneurs alike. Most people can recall times they ignored their gut only to regret it later. Learning to listen to your instinct is a great form of self-preservation. It's both incredibly easy and tough at the same time, but worth the effort to master."
— *Barbara Corcoran*

Have you ever seen someone who seems to have spectacular success, with results so phenomenal that you feel that no matter how hard you work or study, you'll never achieve anything that exciting? No matter how much you save, you'll never buy a house that nice. Or no matter how many business degrees you've earned or business processes you've studied, you'll never have a business that successful or make that much money. Or when you see groundbreaking success like that of Oprah Winfrey, Madam C.J. Walker (one of America's first female self-made millionaires), or Cathy Hughes (founder of RadioOne and TVOne and the first African American woman to head a publicly traded corporation), you can't even begin to figure out what process to put in place to achieve at that level. Well, before you start hating—and even if you are already hating on that person—let me share something with you: you absolutely have access to this level of success. It is a direct result of following your gut, or what I call your professional intuition.

Your professional intuition is the inner knowing that is a direct result of all your studies, experiences, and natural insights. It can be honed and developed. And above all, it can be trusted. In this chapter, you'll learn how to build your professional intuition and how to access it and allow it to guide you to success that is perhaps even bigger and better than you could imagine for yourself.

Here's an example of how my professional intuition led me to success that I hadn't anticipated: In 2009, I was contemplating a decision to move from my beloved city of Chicago, where I lived for 19 years, to metropolitan Washington, DC. And I was a nervous wreck. I loved Chicago. I had wanted to live there since I was a child growing up in Nebraska. It was my home. It was a part of the fabric I used to create the woman I had become. I loved the business culture in the city and had learned how to be successful there. But as several opportunities began to percolate for me in the DC area, I had to admit that my gut was sending signals that I should give some serious thought to the possibility of moving.

After I analyzed the opportunities and the chance of long-term success that I had in both locations, I made the decision to move to DC. Within months of moving I was awarded career-changing projects and found myself sitting at the same table with significant political and professional business leaders whom I could only have dreamed of meeting in Chicago. The business ventures I was involved with experienced exponential growth. I knew that my gut had been right. I was grateful to have listened.

THE POWER OF PROFESSIONAL INTUITION

As important as increasing your knowledge is, it isn't the most powerful tool in an entrepreneur's tool belt. It is a vital component, to be sure, but it is most powerful when it is combined with your gut feeling to form what I call professional intuition, which is your greatest source of guidance, power, and success.

Intuition is a form of intelligence that is beyond the rational mind. It is the ability to acquire knowledge without study or the use of reason. Professional intuition is what happens when your professional knowledge and your instinct work in harmony. It is an information-gathering and decision-making tool that draws on your unique point of view, inner wisdom, purpose, intimate knowledge of your craft, education, and understanding of and empathy for your customer or client.

In addition to committing to lifelong learning and staying abreast of industry trends, professional intuition requires that you create quiet time for yourself and give yourself the space to think clearly and entertain or contemplate alternative perspectives. Because it simply can't be heard as clearly when you are either in the midst of other tasks or forcing a solution. Professional intuition speaks in whispers; it needs quiet to be heard and courage to be acted on.

A gut feeling actually doesn't originate in your abdomen, despite its name. Neuroscientists have identified two areas of the brain—the insula (responsible for social emotions like pride or guilt, and importantly, for regulating our emotions) and the amygdala (which cues our "fight or flight" response to threats)—that send what's known as "somatic markers." These electronic impulses are messages that indicate when something feels right, or it doesn't. One risk of putting too much stock in intellectual study is that you can dismiss or ignore these potent motivational feelings, or somatic markers. But the magic happens when you combine your feelings and your intellectual assessment of the facts—that combination becomes your professional intuition. And the more that you pay attention to the outcome of trusting your professional intuition, the better your decision-making can become. Professional intuition can also help you anticipate future potential problems and develop more effective strategies right from the get-go, once you learn to harness its exquisite power.

I like to think of professional intuition as where my professional instincts, business knowledge, and intellect blend. When you are all in and your instincts, knowledge, and intellect come together it will accelerate your outcomes, help you to devise creative plans and strategies to solve problems, improve and grow your business, and more successfully achieve your business enterprise goals. It will also help you strategize and think several steps ahead, cultivate professional relationships that support your professional goals, anticipate market and industry changes, and better identify how to satisfy your customers and staff. It is a valuable tool that sets you apart from others. It incorporates your authenticity, your purpose, and your intellect. It is the stuff that genius is made of.

CREATING THE SPACE FOR PROFESSIONAL INTUITION TO BUBBLE UP

I often have entrepreneurs who call me looking for a solution to some problem that they're having in their business. They say things like, "I tried staying open later, but it didn't work," or, "I tried paying my staff more, but it didn't work," or even, "I tried changing my approach and nothing worked!" The problem with this scattershot method of attempting to problem solve is that it is based solely on intellect—or worse, on traditional textbook approaches that may no longer be valid in the global digital marketplace. The rational mind will only get you so far. You need your intuition to take you the rest of the way.

Here's how to use the rational and the subconscious minds together: Draw on your knowledge of your product, industry, or service to narrow down your options—not to choose an option but to simply establish what your possibilities are. Once you have distilled the choices, you can then use your gut to make the final call, even—or especially—when you are making decisions in an area where you have little experience to guide you, or where there doesn't appear to be a clear winner among your available options.

The best way to hear what your gut is trying to tell you is to still the mind and get quiet. In other words, meditate. As a busy entrepreneur this can be a tough task. Even though I've meditated for years, I have a tough time when I'm busy. So, I build meditation or quiet time into my schedule. No matter what I'm doing, I stop at a specific time each day to meditate. If I run into a difficulty, I take a moment to stop and meditate. My grandmother had an antidote for every ailment that always included the phrase, "Get somewhere and sit down." Whether you fell down, got dumped by a teen crush, or had a stomach ache, getting somewhere and sitting down was always a part of her prescription. I have come to realize as an adult that that prescription still works. So, if you can't get past the concept of meditating, just get somewhere quiet and sit down for a few minutes. When you commit to a meditative practice, you accelerate your intuitive ability and you create a conscious process through which you can seek clarity and get answers.

I started practicing meditation when I was a business consultant many years ago. When I was challenged to work through complicated problems or dilemmas for which I had no immediate logical answer or solution, I'd sit with the problem and pose questions to myself. I would actually say the questions out loud, and then sit in silence without trying to come up with an instantaneous solution. After 10 minutes or so, I'd move on to another task. But remarkably, when I would later revisit the problem, I always had a brand-new way to approach it, or a novel perspective that would lead to a viable solution. This process is bankable; you can count on it. It works every single time.

Your quiet time doesn't have to be meditation—it could be yoga, CrossFit, mountain climbing. Whatever activity gets your mind to a quieter place will help. To get the most out of these endeavors, think of the problem you're facing before you head into yoga class or sit down to meditate. Ask yourself the questions you'd like the answers to out loud beforehand. Then devote your full attention to whatever activity you've chosen. When you sit back down to contemplate the problem, I guarantee that an entirely new way of looking at the challenge will bubble up in your mind and lead the way to an elegant solution.

Of course, in order to get this mental downtime, you've got to give yourself some space in your schedule for non-work-related activities. You need time to re-group; you can't always work like a dog. I know that our culture prizes working hard above all else—especially for entrepreneurs—but if you don't take time to quiet your mind regularly, you'll risk burnout or meltdown, whatever you prefer to call it. In the short run, however, failure to take quiet time may mean that you'll miss elements of your business that may be critical to mitigating risks, forecasting, or simply showing empathy to your staff and customers. Remember, your professional intuition is your edge and you need quiet time to develop your edge. Not only will going constantly prevent you from accessing your professional intuition, it may very well land you in the hospital or make you feel like this whole entrepreneur thing is simply too hard. And when that happens, you are very likely to end up right back where you started—marginalized.

ADDING ENERGY INTO THE EQUATION

As an entrepreneur, you must learn to be responsible for the attitude and point of view that you bring to your business, negotiations, hiring, policies, processes, and concepts. Your thoughts and your mental stance taken together add up to your energy—the subtle vibrations that infuse and emanate off every living thing. Your energy influences your professional intuition: Thinking low-energy thoughts, such as being jealous of another's success, or angry because you perceive that someone is trying to take something from you, will cause you to see only choices that perpetuate that low-energy state. Assuming a high-energy stance of rising above the competition and seeking to deliver and create value for your customers, yourself, and the world at large, will help you see and realize high-energy solutions.

Being responsible for your own energy is a must. It requires knowledge, intuition, creativity, and intention. Whatever message you send to your staff or to your customers will dictate how they will respond and feel about you as an entrepreneurial leader.

Becoming sensitive to energy gives you another assessment tool to add to your professional intuition toolbox. I can sense the energy of my staff and my customers; I then use that assessment to guide how I manage my employees and interact with my customers.

When a customer walks into a retail store, for example, they feel a certain way. They may not be able to articulate how they feel, or why they feel it, but they feel it nonetheless. That's because they are sensing the energy of the business itself as well as the people who run it and who staff it. And how they feel determines how much they will spend on your goods and services. Whether they visit a spa or consult with an attorney, for example, they feel the energy and intention of the owner or management via the energy of the person who greets them or answers the phone. When you go to a concert, you feel the supernatural rock star energy of the artist. Many are willing to pay hundreds of dollars for the feeling that the artist gives them. As an entrepreneur, you must focus on creating good feelings and high levels of energy and satisfaction for your customers.

How do you present to the people you aim to serve? Is your appearance attractive and in line with industry standards? If you violate industry standards as it relates to your attire or overall look, are you prepared to mitigate the risks that this violation creates in terms of customer appreciation and overall satisfaction? At the Vascular Surgery Center that I have helped to build and develop, we have staff members who are often much younger than the average demographic we serve (the majority of the patients are over 60). After carefully studying that age demographic to learn what makes them comfortable and more open to a pleasant experience, we made the decision to require the staff to dress in branded uniforms and garments. This gives the appearance of order and compliance that is attractive to our patient demographic, and something that, as a group, these patients have come to expect through their own experience. We have guidelines about piercings and tattoos for this same reason. You and your employees have to balance authenticity with approachability to show respect for your clients. And your professional intuition will help you strike that balance and give you the confidence to set those standards, even if they might be unpopular with your staff.

Any time you are faced with an important choice—which, let's be honest, is nearly every day—remember that your ability to tap into your professional intuition is what makes phenomenal success possible. Consulting your professional intuition at every step of the way will help you to catapult your business and career into the stratosphere. Learn to get quiet and listen to it!

CHAPTER 6

DEFINE SUCCESS FOR YOURSELF: AVOID THE PERILS OF THE COMPETITIVE MIND

"Every person who becomes rich by competition knocks down the ladder by which he/she rises, and keeps others down, but every person who gets rich by creation opens a way for others to follow and inspires them to do so." — Wallace D. Wattles, The Science of Getting Rich

This quote was written almost 100 years ago. At the time, this concept that competition wasn't the end-all, be-all was so controversial that it was only discussed in secret societies of so-called elites. Only now, 100 years later, is the world conceptually evolving out of the mindset where success is defined by how tall we stand over others, or how much power we wield over them. But there are many beliefs—and tangible evidence of those beliefs in the form of racial and financial divides—that still need to be undone so that more of us can embrace collaboration as the order of the day, and not strictly competition.

Today's world was not built on equality but on the ego of people who felt they had to hold others down in order to be successful. In an effort to thrive in this world, many people have built their personalities on the spirit of competition and completely identified themselves by their ability to have the latest and greatest possessions and, most insidiously, to keep others from having what they have. This approach worked for a time. For whatever reason, it was something that the laws of the universe permitted. But—news flash!—a focus on competition is no longer the dominant path to success. To the contrary, a competitive mind is becoming more and more of a hindrance to success.

In business today, it's the partnerships and collaborations that are responsible for creating record-breaking sales. Co-branding and outsourcing help to increase access to more customers, mitigate risks, expand market footprints, and create unique products and services. If you are trying to guard your turf and do everything on your own you are going to lose out.

I had a colleague recently say to me, "I'm old school, I have a problem with everyone being equal." When he made that statement, I had a light bulb moment. Think about that for a minute. We have all been forced to operate from or subjected to the mindset that sets the young and old, black and white, fat and skinny in furious competition with one another. But this is no longer a mindset that can successfully carry us into the changing world that is being advanced by technology in every industry.

This addiction to competition is an integral reason why so many of us are marginalized in the first place. Remember, marginalization is a tool used to deny members of a certain group the same rights as everyone else. Whether you're African American and it's socially acceptable for you to be shot down in the street, or you're a middle-aged professional and it's no surprise when you are forced out of your job and replaced by a younger and less experienced lower wage worker; marginalization is a tool often used to create competition that ultimately eliminates the opportunities and rights of those who "lose."

But marginalization also opens up new markets and opportunities for collaboration and partnerships. Entrepreneurial businesses that solve the problems created by marginalization—or avoid them altogether—are some of the largest business ventures today. Companies like Uber and Lyft give people who are marginalized by limited access to transportation or are squeezed out of more traditional job markets access to a product or a revenue stream that enhances quality of life for both the client and service provider. Marginalizing the senior population opens the door for new businesses that help to solve problems that historically would have crippled this group. But if you are focused on the marginalization itself and feeling upset that the old ways of doing things have been taken away, you won't see those possibilities.

THE INDIVIDUAL DANGERS OF THE COMPETITIVE MINDSET

I realize that the non-desirability of competitiveness is a tough lesson to swallow. (I have received plenty of pushback in the comments of my blog posts where I espouse my point of view that the era in which competition is the driving force of success is over.) Many of you in business are really struggling with this concept because we have been taught that competition is the very heart of business and the foundation of our self-worth. Don't get me wrong, competition has its place. But creativity, problem-solving, and branding have replaced competition as the dominant forces that fuel extraordinary success, extreme customer loyalty, and record-setting profits.

I too was taught early in my career that business was all about competition. We were given examples in college of companies creating competing brands and the importance of studying the competition. And while these are important business concepts, they should not consume us. Of course another business can come along with a better product or a more cost-effective way to deliver a service and thus create a problem for your business. The question is whether or not your reaction is to become more creative and responsive to your customer, to copy your competitor, or to set out to destroy your competitor. There is only one sustainable solution in that set of choices—do you have the open-mindedness to see which one it is?

THINKING BEYOND POP CULTURE

Pop culture is defined as a way of life transmitted via the mass media and aimed particularly at younger people. I see countless entrepreneurs who are unable to identify the difference between a corporate business strategy and pop culture trends. Moreover, they are unable to measure the effect of these trends on how they deliver goods and services and mitigate risks within their business. This creates blind spots that limit their ability to identify the strengths and weaknesses of industry trends, tap into new markets, and reach out to subcultures that can be converted into viable, loyal customers. The focus that modern pop culture places on competition can be crippling to an entrepreneur who is blindly following the herd.

In pop culture we see artists and entertainers competing with and battling against one another for media attention, so we tend to subconsciously adopt this behavior as a way of life. We live in a society that has thrived on competition. We compete so that we can be better than the next person. We compete because we are afraid to lose. Many of us are victims of discrimination or racism and must work hard to change our competitive mentality lest we either evolve into our abusers or live perpetual lives as victims. Our competitive mindset is often our downfall. And in the case of modern pop culture, our downfall is often the mindset imposed upon us by mass media.

THE PERILS OF THE COMPETITIVE MIND

If you try to take the shortcut of copying others in order to compete, you are doomed to be defeated or quite embarrassed. I had a personal situation where I was teaching a course with another business leader. At the time I was speaking regularly on the power of authenticity; my talks were constructed principally from the wisdom my mother passed down to me and my brother. She consistently taught us early to never be followers; her teachings were the inspiration for my Authenticity Movement™. The talks also drew upon my experiences and studies of emotional intelligence, spiritual traditions I have studied, and my unique personal corporate business experiences. I laughed literally out loud as the speaker before me, in her attempt to compete against me, included quotes from my mother and examples from my corporate experiences in her presentation and represented them as an original theory that she created. Little did she know, over half of the audience knew me personally (the organization was once a client and the organizers were former business partners). You can probably imagine her embarrassment as my colleagues laughed and later explained to her how they knew she had tried to pass off my material as her own.

Don't get me wrong, the saying that there is nothing new under the sun is more true than not. And being inspired by others and studying successful people provides great building blocks to augment and hone your own professional intuition. But to become so insecure that you completely steal someone else's personal brand is not only lame, but gives the very competitors that you fear an insight into your lack of creativity.

Other perils of the competitive mind include:

- Comparing yourself to others is a recipe for depression because you know all your foibles and downfalls but likely only see the external successes of your competition.
- Being too intensely competitive steers you toward a more external focus where you lose control of your direction.
- If you are consumed by being competitive you are almost always playing catch-up or chasing something or someone else; you are reacting and playing defense and ignoring the power of innovation.
- It makes you focused on keeping score instead of building your business.
- When you are competitive you take your eye off the purposeful innovation that can help you create your vision, instead spending all your energy on just being better than the next person.
- Competition breeds jealousy, causes you to rush to judgment, and makes it difficult for you to form partnerships that are so often vital for entrepreneurs.

- It contributes to impatience and causes you to start looking for shortcuts and making poor decisions due to a false sense of urgency.

THE END OF MAJORITY RULE

There is hopeful evidence that this old competition-is-king mindset won't work much longer. The Census Bureau states that 38% of the United States was considered minority in 2014 and that by 2060 56% will be considered minority. Beyond race, when you consider how many people are handicapped, veterans, senior citizens, or chronically ill, you have close to an entire population that can be considered marginalized. The recent student-driven movement for gun legislation shows that even our youth across the economic and social board are marginalized.

The Census Bureau itself says that "no group will have a majority share of the total and the United States will become a plurality nation of racial and ethnic groups." What that means to me is that as entrepreneurs we can't afford to discriminate if we want to be profitable. We can't exclude anyone because no group has the power of majority any more. There is nowhere to hide.

What it also means is that when we are freed from the idea that the biggest herd wins, we no longer have to focus on blending in—in fact, standing out is now a strength and a virtue. By embracing who we are and allowing our creativity to flourish we will learn that we are all different and alike. It is our individual uniqueness and authenticity that will take us to that next level. There is no one else like you. Own your individuality; don't throw that away trying to be like someone else! It will eat at your soul and cause you to leave money on the table because you won't be focused on delivering the service and experience that only you can provide. More importantly, it will prevent you from developing and strengthening your professional intuition.

Certainly, there will always be those who have and those who don't, but it is no longer spiritually chic or financially intelligent to put energy into keeping down those who are struggling or crushing people for their shortcomings and downfalls. See, at the end of the day, none of us are "all that." And no one is truly better or more worthy of opportunity than anyone else. So, to put someone else down is to put yourself down. There are more so-called marginalized people who are self-made millionaires and billionaires today than ever before. A study conducted by Fidelity Investments found that 86% of today's millionaires are self-made and did not consider themselves wealthy growing up.

Today's successful businesses offer services and products to everyone with the appropriate means to acquire them. Not only does this change the energy of the business world and create more opportunities, it also gives entrepreneurs greater access to more customers, and more diverse ones at that. The internet has helped to bring about a global economic structure that has revolutionized the way in which we do business in this world. The old way of thinking where businesses would block the efforts of others and withhold knowledge, opportunity, and access to products and services is no longer a secret key to success.

Those who are creative, who respect diversity, and who think outside the box will be granted the gift of success. I call this "thinking without borders." Being able to think outside the box is one of the greatest benefits of professional intuition. According to McKinsey & Company research, companies in the top quartile for gender or racial and ethnic diversity are more likely to have financial returns above their national industry medians. Companies in the bottom quartile in these dimensions are statistically less likely to achieve above average returns.

Entrepreneurs who embrace the power of inclusiveness and diversity tap into a richly spiritual power that bestows upon them the responsibility of abundance and wealth. And I don't mean success defined solely by money. I mean success defined by the advancement of mind, body, and soul.

As an entrepreneur in the healthcare sector, I focus my staff on our purpose. We don't blindly deliver service like robots or treat our patients like widgets in a factory. Everything we do has a purpose; from the way we have orchestrated the patient experience to the contracts we negotiate with our vendors, we seek to treat everyone with humanity. I can attest the more you focus on a purpose that extends beyond profits, the more successful you'll be. And as you develop your professional intuition, you will see more opportunities to gain market share, increase profits, mitigate risks, and better serve your customers.

After all, you were born into this world for a reason. It makes sense that the universe or God would reward you for tapping into your purpose. The path to your purpose starts with accepting who you are and being yourself. Those who are fortunate enough to generate and possess wealth will be those who open the way for others to follow.

CREATIVITY IS THE NEW BUSINESS CURRENCY

For many of us, our growth is stunted because our actions are motivated by whether or not we believe that we can or cannot "compete." That is the root concept behind those who are "haters." They see the success of someone else and immediately make it about themselves. They are keeping score and get upset because they have decided that you are winning. This insecurity or emotion overwhelms them and they begin to make behavioral choices based on what they feel.

It's very natural and human to be afraid of failure. But what we fail to realize is that there is an alternative to being competitive—it is to be creative. Creativity enables innovative breakthroughs, changes old business models, attracts and retains customers, sets trends, and allows us to create businesses that align with our own personal authenticity. Creativity makes you incomparable.

Focusing on your creativity can give you more courage and increase your market share. You can also create new markets and render the competition irrelevant. It is very difficult to even compare two extremely creative people to each other. It's like trying to compare Prince to Michael Jackson or Whitney Houston to Chaka Khan. While they may have the same profession, their individual and incredibly unique marks on their industry are incomparable.

Many of us are so tired and so overwhelmed with life. The fatigue is brought on by the fact that we've either veered off course or never even had a game plan of our own in the first place. Chasing competitors is exhausting. But creating is exhilarating. There is nothing more mentally orgasmic than seeing something that started in your head come to fruition. Being competitive creates a resistance that is exhausting. Resistance is often the root cause of stress. And we all know the perils of excessive amounts of stress or, in this case, excessive amounts of resistance.

Instead of focusing on being creative so that we tap into our own purpose, we spend hours mimicking what our so-called competitors are doing. We often watch characters on television and say, "I want to be just like that." We can count on one hand the ideas we've had that originated from our own creative flow. The way we wear our hair, the clothes we wear, and the way we act are all based on what we've seen others do. And we do it because we don't have a sense of uniqueness or belief in our own ideas. Our creative muscles are weak to the point that they are almost paralyzed.

Being creative requires that you take responsibility for your life and your business plan. It means that you use your struggle and the pain of marginalization to ignite your creativity, fuel your determination, and solve problems that only a marginalized person would be able to identify and solve. It's not just good for your soul, it's good for your bottom line too: a study by Adobe and Forrester Consulting found that 82% of companies believe there is a strong connection between creativity and positive business results. In fact, companies that foster creative thinking outperform their rivals in revenue growth, market share, and competitive leadership.

Here are some steps that you can take to help you evolve out of the competitive ego mind and cultivate your creativity:

- **Don't focus obsessively on being impressive:** Your uniqueness is impressive. The next time you are talking to someone, refrain from statements or conversations that are designed to impress that person. Try not to show off or over-talk him or her. Instead, focus on encouraging others and actively listening. This will help you to determine when it is truly time for you to focus on being impressive—with your actions as well as your words.

- **Stop talking about people:** We are all guilty of this. There are times when discussing a person's behavior is necessary. But most of the time we sit around and blast other people for no reason other than to make ourselves feel good—this is nothing more than the competitive mind at work. If you find yourself in this behavioral cycle, just be quiet. If you can't think of anything good to say or find anything better to do than to sit around and analyze the behavior of others, try analyzing your own behavior. My mother always said that what often bothers you about other people is what bothers other people about you.

- **Practice gratitude:** Gratitude is defined as "the state of being grateful." A state is a condition of mind or temperament. The magical effects of gratitude involve shifting our mental consciousness to focus on what we have as opposed to what we don't have. Gratitude is the manner through which we relate to and acknowledge the power that gives us everything we need and desire. If we are focused on our own blessings, we will shift from the competitive mindset and will be too busy and too grateful to ruin it by focusing on energy-depleting competition.

- **Stop trying to be an island:** Develop relationships, share ideas, and ask for and offer support; the entrepreneurial business landscape is more complex than ever before, which means (a) there are more opportunities than ever before, and (b) no one person or company—or philosophy—holds all the "keys" to success. Collaboration is the key.

> **Focus on the experience you provide first, and the product or service you use to deliver it second**

One thing I say to my staff constantly is, "It's all about the experience." After studying and diligently applying emotional intelligence to my life, I realized that much of business is not directly about the product or service that's delivered—it's the experience of how that product or service is delivered that matters.

A good experience attracts loyal customers who are willing to pay a premium for that experience and who will tell others about it. People will pay for a good experience, sometimes even if the product is mediocre. How many times have you gone to a restaurant or purchased a designer bag just because of how it made you feel, even if the food or product wasn't all that great? Most people will readily exchange money for a delightful experience.

This is important for entrepreneurs to understand. If people have a good experience with you, you are more likely to get repeat business. And a "good experience" does not mean that you have to act like a cheerleader or tell an excessive amount of jokes. I define a "good experience" as one where you add value. You want to move through life looking to create a good experience by providing additional value to everyone and every situation you are in. Focusing on delivering value will also naturally help you turn your attention away from competition. Get grounded in what you have to offer and who you are and you will create an experience that your competitors will be hard pressed to duplicate.

At the end of the day, competition is an illusion. This is why it's so exhausting—it's like chasing a mirage that is constantly receding just as you think you're about to reach it.

Remember, you are here for a reason that was designed specifically by your Creator. So what is for you is for you only and what is for someone else is for them, and there is nothing either of you can do about it. Navigate your way out of the emotions caused by living a life dominated by insecurity and competition. It takes emotional intelligence to heal from old wounds and develop confidence in yourself and your future. It takes emotional strength to access alternative ways of thinking and to avoid falling victim to a mindset obsessed with competition. In the next chapter, I'll cover how to develop your emotional intelligence so that you make better decisions, take results-oriented actions, and trust in your own abilities and prospects so that you can create success on your own terms.

CHAPTER 7

THE RESILIENT MIND: DEVELOP YOUR EMOTIONAL INTELLIGENCE

"Entrepreneurship is a form of art; it's a form of expression. It lets you be who you want to be, it lets you inspire others to get behind a vision, and it allows you to give back in a way you've never given back before. It will test you; it will take every ounce of your energy and your emotion to succeed at it. Entrepreneurship can change the world. It's life's greatest test. It's your legacy." — *Tim Denning,* Addicted2Success

I have always loved music, art and dance. As a child I played piano, organ, and flute; I sang, danced, and loved to paint and draw. As a student I remember always feeling forced to choose between STEM subjects and liberal arts. This was especially difficult for me because I loved and excelled at both, so being boxed in to one or another always bothered me.

What I later came to realize is that the box I felt the world was trying to place me in was a carefully crafted web of emotions that I had developed during a lifetime of trying to manage societal, cultural, and parental pressures. It was a strategy that I had been unconsciously developing—on my own—my entire life. I was able to tweak that strategy with tools I learned and developed as I became more emotionally intelligent, and I came to see that I was the only person who had the power to keep me in any one box. When I learned the importance of teaching people how to treat me, setting personal intentions, and being more aware of how my actions affected others, I finally took control of my life and my business success truly took off.

I've watched countless entrepreneurs over the years sabotage their own success because of their inability to manage their emotions. In this chapter, I hope to help you shortcut through some of that arduous growth process by shining a light on how to grow spiritually and emotionally through the process of increasing your emotional intelligence quotient (EQ).

One of the most important skills an entrepreneur can cultivate is resilience—the ability to withstand or recover quickly from difficult situations and adapt to change. And the best way to build your resilience is to strengthen your emotional intelligence. I share this information with you now, because the truth is that you will face challenging situations on your path to building a business that honors your whole self and creates financial stability for you and perhaps even your children. Perhaps you already are. And maybe those challenges seem insurmountable.

The beauty of emotional intelligence is that it helps you navigate difficult situations with grace, savvy, and strength, and to do it in a manner that focuses on attracting the next project, business, or opportunity. With emotional intelligence, failure really doesn't exist anymore—it's just a doorway to a new opportunity that's a better fit and a way to gauge the quality of your thoughts.

You can still be successful if you ignore the effect of your emotions on your choices and decisions, but you can avoid some potentially dangerous setbacks if your strategy includes emotional awareness.

EMOTIONAL INTELLIGENCE HELPS YOU HANDLE ALL SETBACKS ESPECIALLY THE BIGGEST ONES

Even before I had ever heard of the concept of emotional intelligence, I used it clumsily to overcome difficulty and to think outside of the box. It helped me through even the direst circumstances: I was homeless twice and lost everything I owned three times. Yes, that means I had to start over completely from scratch three different times.

The first time I was homeless I was in my 20s. I left Nebraska as a new college graduate and landed in Indianapolis where I held several jobs, including as a waitress, commercial insurance underwriter, and a staff accountant for a big firm. Along the way I found myself homeless after a disagreement with a relative. I went to several interviews wearing the only suit I had and nowhere to live. At that time all I knew was determination and resilience. In a nutshell, there was no way in hell I was going to give up.

In order to keep going, I would shut down all emotions and force my mind into radio silence. I even avoided talking about the challenges I was facing with anyone until recently. I was definitely scared, but I was more determined. I felt that dealing with the family gossip about me or thinking about what my friends from college were saying would only weaken me and make the process too overwhelming. So, I just got quiet and started working and focusing on what I wanted and how I wanted to construct my life. It was the first time that I remember consciously thinking about how emotions would affect my decisions, for better or for worse.

I continued to struggle through my early 30s, sometimes facing tragedy because I avoided an emotionally difficult situation and other times because I didn't understand my emotional triggers. Back then I was all about avoiding at any cost what I called emotional drama. I was terrible at teaching people how to treat me. I was always upset when people didn't see me or didn't treat me in a manner that I thought I deserved. I didn't realize that I couldn't change other people and that I could only change myself and my reactions.

My number one motivation was to be a winner, but my underlying unhappiness was rooted in the fact that I defined being a winner according to the reaction I received from others. So, despite numerous triumphs and successes, I still functioned from a place of defeat.

Many of my strategies and actions were an attempt to protect my feelings and score points for protecting others. When I began to study emotional intelligence, it became clear to me how my emotions had affected my decisions, limited my success, and negatively impacted my happiness.

After hitting what I considered a plateau, I began to focus on what I could do to break through the limits that sometimes were self-inflicted and other times were created by a culture, society, and business environment that did not nurture a black woman trying to be a winner in business and especially as an entrepreneur. I finally had a healthy six-figure income in an office where I was constantly overlooked and mistaken for the corporate cleaning lady. Meaning, I was good enough to fix all the problems but never good enough to create solutions and processes on the front end. I felt my life being threatened by mediocrity and stagnation. I saw myself settling into a routine that was centered on safety and security that avoided risk and change. I had finally figured out that what I was craving was creativity. But I didn't know how to change the trajectory of my life because I was afraid to tap into the passion and power that I had unconsciously learned to suppress in my 20s. Even though I knew that creativity was what I craved, I was afraid, because creativity ignites emotions that I had spent a lifetime trying to avoid. Along the way, I had connected creativity with poverty, e.g., a starving artist.

What I ultimately realized was that I was not doing a good job at representing myself. I didn't speak my truth because, at that time, emotional intelligence to me meant avoiding emotions and emotionally charged situations. Despite being a creative person, I was rarely creative. So, I rarely communicated my desires and shared my point of view. I had several hints over the years that emotional intelligence was the key. I first heard Anthony Robbins teach on it. I then began to study Daniel Goleman, who is known as the father of emotional intelligence. I took a deeper dive and completed a certification course in EQ. I read every book that I could find on the subject. It wasn't until becoming a certified emotional intelligence coach that I finally learned to manage my own emotions.

> **Learning how to deal with my emotions with compassion and skill completely changed my life—and it can change yours, too.**

CULTIVATING EMOTIONAL INTELLIGENCE CUTS BOTH WAYS: IT HELPS YOU AND YOUR CLIENT

If people don't trust you or don't like you, they won't give you their hard-earned money. Conversely, if they trust you, they will be more likely to look to you for guidance. It's as simple as that.

Most entrepreneurs don't make the connection between success and emotional intelligence—especially entrepreneurs who have transitioned from technician to business owner. They tend to focus on the fact that they are really good technicians, or experts in their field. While that is an awesome characteristic, it's not the be-all and end-all. It can keep you stuck in a creative vacuum, for one. And, more importantly, customers will patronize a lesser technician in exchange for a better experience or relationship. You could say, "Hey they've got better pizza down the street," and the customer will say, "Yes, but Papa Joe is my man. I like him so I get my pizza from him."

Establishing trust and eliciting positive emotions are what highly effective advertising is all about—it's not really publicizing the product or service; it's about making you feel a certain way about that corporation. The vast majority of advertising is about building an emotional connection, fostering feelings of trust and affection for the company that's doing the advertising. The relationship and experience are just as important as the product or service itself. And your emotions dictate the quality of your interactions and your relationships.

Raising your emotional intelligence also helps you create a better experience for your customers—an important strategy that I covered in Chapter 6. Because in order to provide a satisfying experience, you must have the ability to imagine how your service, product, and method of delivery will make your customer feel. Raising your emotional intelligence helps everyone—you, your customer, and everyone you have a relationship with.

> **If your emotional abilities aren't in hand, if you don't have self-awareness, if you are not able to manage your distressing emotions, if you can't have empathy and have effective relationships, then no matter how smart you are, you are not going to get very far. — Daniel Goleman**

THE IMPORTANCE OF GOING DEEP

Before I go further into the specifics of what emotional intelligence is and how you can develop it, I want to stress the importance of learning to drill down past the surface when you are seeking to grow emotionally. Going deep into the dark abyss of emotions can be frightening. Many of us stay on the surface because we are literally too lazy, arrogant, or afraid to face the fears that block our success. It's much easier to decorate the barriers that are holding us back, or ignore them altogether. And in most cases, that's exactly what we do.

After many years of attending motivational seminars and posting affirmations and quotes around my home, all of which are helpful tools, I realized that in order to experience life-altering progress, I needed to examine myself on a much deeper level. I'd leave the seminars and workshops feeling fired up only to realize that all my affirmations were the equivalent of putting a Band-Aid on a deep wound.

Many people mistakenly think that emotional intelligence is all about emotional control or about not having emotions at all. Nothing could be further from the truth. Emotions are your compass. They help you to figure out when you are on the path of alignment, and when you are on a path of destruction. Don't let this frighten you. One quick rule of thumb is that if you feel good as you contemplate or take a specific action, you are closer to your authentic path than if you feel bad or have misgivings while thinking about it or doing it. If you focus on negativity, you are further away than if you focus on positivity. If you focus positively on what you want, you are closer than if you focus negatively on what you don't want.

IS EQ (EMOTIONAL INTELLIGENCE) MORE IMPORTANT THAN IQ?

The simple answer to the above question is "yes." Without a doubt. After all, IQ only measures a very narrow section of cognitive ability. According to Daniel Goleman, best-selling author of Emotional Intelligence, Primal Leadership, and several other groundbreaking books, "Many studies show that the old concepts of IQ revolved around a narrow band of linguistic and math skills and that doing well on IQ tests was most directly a predictor of success in the classroom or as a professor but less and less so as one's life path diverges from the academic arena." On the other hand, emotional intelligence informs and affects all aspects of your life—your personal happiness and well-being as well as your business and financial success.

When you allow your emotional intelligence to be compromised, you lessen your intuitive flow and limit your ability to make decisions and think critically. This hinders your ability to cope with and find your way out of difficult situations. If you are challenged by something and you think that your only option is something that scares you, you might give up. But if you can think through alternative options, methods, or strategies, you are more likely to be successful.

During my plateau period, I took an IQ test for a major position with a large company. My results showed that my IQ was well above average. But if I was so smart, why weren't my life and my level of success also well above average? Don't get me wrong. I was doing reasonably well at the time. But I had hit a plateau and I wanted more. When I humbled myself and began to assess my EQ, I saw for the first time the blind spots that had plagued me for years—my inability to see how my choices and decisions were affected by my emotions. Learning to work more skillfully with my emotions led me to make better choices and to further develop my professional intuition, and it will do the same for you, too.

EMOTIONAL INTELLIGENCE DEFINED

In simple terms, emotional intelligence is commonly defined as the ability to determine what makes us happy, what makes us sad, and how to change the emotions we are feeling. When you raise your EQ, you can discover what choices led to your specific emotional state and how to change your emotional state so that you can approach your life and your business from a more positive place. While IQ (intelligence quotient) remains relatively fixed throughout one's lifetime, EQ can be effectively and positively raised by learning and practicing new skills at any time. By understanding EQ, you can expand your self-awareness and use emotions to your advantage. So let's get you on the track to a higher EQ, shall we?

The five main domains of emotional intelligence (derived from the chapter "When Smart Is Dumb" in the book Emotional Intelligence by Daniel Goldman) are:

1. **Knowing Your Emotions.** Otherwise known as self-awareness, this fundamental piece of emotional intelligence is being able to recognize a feeling as it happens. This ability is also the mother of all consciousness. For me this means being clear on how I feel about things and understanding how and why I react in a specific manner. This helps to create certainty and clarity and make more well-informed plans and decisions. For example, I noticed that one of my staff members got extremely nervous whenever she had to discuss money. Her voice would rise an octave and her speech became choppy. She was always visibly nervous about asking clients to pay for services or discussing payment plans. She never realized how nervous she got until we discussed it. She initially denied being nervous about it, primarily because she was completely unaware of her emotions during financial transactions. We started the simple task of her being more consciously aware of her body, voice, and thoughts whenever she had to discuss finances with a client. This exercise was

an incredible eye opener for her. It revealed a blind spot that she now could begin to develop a strategy to overcome.

2. **Managing Emotions.** Handling feelings so they are appropriate is an ability that builds on self-awareness. This has to do with the capacity to soothe oneself, to shake off rampant anxiety, gloom, irritability, and to handle disappointment and the consequences of failure.

   Take that same employee who experienced extreme anxiety when it came to discussing finances. Once she became aware of her emotions she now could begin the task of managing those emotions. Together we examined the inner conversation she would have with herself during these client discussions. What she discovered was that she was already anticipating a negative or even combative outcome from a client. This terrified her, but it was all in her head. She was reacting to a story—a false narrative—that she was telling herself. She literally would say to herself, "This person is going to yell at me for talking about money, they're going to say no, I'm going to be a failure, they're not going to like me." She began to see how this self-talk made it easier for her to avoid the conversation and ultimately affected her sales numbers. We spent some time changing this internal conversation to something that changed her emotional reaction and allowed her to manage those adverse emotions as they arose. Simply thinking about her past successes helped her to gain confidence that she could be successful; and realizing that a negative client reaction wasn't about her personally helped her to remove herself from the equation and reduce her fear of disappointment or rejection.

3. **Motivating Yourself.** Marshalling emotions in the service of a worthy goal is essential for paying attention, for self-motivation and achieving mastery, and for creativity. Emotional self-control, which includes delaying gratification and stifling impulsiveness, underlies accomplishment of every sort. And being

able to get into the flow state enables outstanding performance of all kinds.

Learning to motivate myself meant that I became more disciplined, consistent, and focused. This helped me to increase my productivity and create more precise plans. When I started down this road of being my own boss, I knew that being disciplined was a critical aspect of my success. So, despite the emotions associated with fatigue or just not wanting to get out of bed, I set a schedule for myself that I stuck to. I thought that if I worked for someone else I'd likely have to work 9 a.m. to 5 p.m., so whether I had a boss or not I was going to stay in that mode and report to myself. I kept my office open during those business hours whether I had clients or not, even if I was not there. My goal of building an institution motivated me to maintain structure, form, processes, and policies in my business.

4. Recognizing Emotions in Others. **Empathy, another mental** ability that builds on emotional awareness, is the fundamental people skill. Empathy kindles altruism and engenders others' trust in you. It also minimizes the social costs of being emotionally tone deaf. This is especially critical in business since the most successful businesses are those that solve problems. If you find a problem in your community and you can work to build a business that solves it, you will enjoy the double benefits of profiting with a purpose.

Understanding the emotions of others helps to build productive relationships. I remember having one employee who was exceptionally talented. I would often give her the most challenging projects and client conversations, ask her to stay late or come in early to handle meeting prep while I was out in the field at meetings. Despite her insistence that she wanted to do it, I was aware that she was rarely home with her family. I noticed she was not as well put together as she had once been. So, despite her protests, I built some time into the schedule to allow her to give herself and her family more attention. It was a matter of putting myself in her shoes.

5. **Handling Relationships.** The art of building strong relationships relies on your skill in managing emotions in others. These are the abilities that undergird popularity, leadership, and interpersonal effectiveness. Handling relationships has become a tool that I find important especially when I'm managing multiple projects with a lot of moving parts. I find that regular and open communication both with the team and individuals is a viable tool to handling relationships. On large construction projects, for example, it's important to have timely team meetings to discuss issues openly and to address any issues that team members are experiencing or are concerned about. This helps to ensure that team members are having the desired experience on a project, as well as receiving positive and helpful feedback. It lets the team know that you are accessible and concerned about the project and their experience. I make sure that I am regularly present on the site, if possible. This helps me to relate to my team members. When I see them working, I gain a greater appreciation for them personally and not just the work they produce. I can look at work conditions, put myself in their shoes, and make changes that will make things more efficient and help to improve both their productivity and their job satisfaction.

THE BIGGEST OBSTACLES TO DEVELOPING EQ

There are what I call "emotional operations issues" that can make us throw all that great theory out of the window and lose our heads. Here are the three most common ways in which our practice of emotional intelligence can go out of the window.

EMOTIONAL HIJACK

To me this is one of the most brilliant concepts in the discipline. An old adage says that life is 10% of what happens to you and 90% of how you respond to it. Again, another great theory. But when you think of it in terms of emotional hijacking, you can better understand, operationally, what this means. Emotional hijacking is a term coined by Daniel Goleman in his excellent book Emotional Intelligence. The term describes changes that occur in the brain and body when we experience excessively high emotions, otherwise known as emotional arousal. So, basically, something happens and you lose it, whether consciously or subconsciously. That event knocks you off your square and sends you into what is commonly known as "fight or flight"—the physiological reaction that occurs in response to a perceived harmful event, attack, or threat to survival. You may not even know what happened to trigger your fight or flight response, and find yourself fighting or running away, either literally or figuratively, because your heightened emotions hijacked you psychologically and even physically, and often spiritually as well. This is often an extremely dangerous state of mind.

The key way to handle emotional hijack is to lean on your skills of emotional awareness and to use that awareness to change your emotional state to one that better serves your purpose. This may involve cooling off, taking a breather, praying, meditating, or going for a walk. Either way, you want to be able to recognize the onset of that emotionally hijacked state of mind and respond accordingly.

When I hit my professional plateau, I realized that my susceptibility to emotional hijack was one of my biggest impediments. I hated the feeling of getting upset, so I avoided highly charged and challenging emotional situations. To this day I can't stand to be around people who are extremely reactive and who act out with a reckless disregard for others.

In order to get out from under the thumb of emotional hijack, I had to first admit that I was an extremely sensitive person. And that much to my dislike, I am very affected by the emotional states of others. I began to use quiet time and meditation to refocus. There are times when I will sit quietly for 5 or 10 minutes several times throughout the day.

I also use strategic planning as a tool to help me navigate emotional hijack. If I've created a plan that I've bought into, I refer back to the plan regularly in an effort to change my mental and emotional state. I use music or personal affirmations to bring myself back on point and into positive focus. I also use extreme workouts like CrossFit or boot camp classes to help me practice quickly changing my mental state and overcome emotional hijacking so that I can get through the challenging workout, for example. When I'm working out, lots of emotions tend to percolate, and depending upon where I am on that emotional scale, those emotions can make it either easy or difficult to get through the workout. They also empower me to develop the skills and the stamina I can then use when I encounter emotional hijack.

EMOTIONAL BLACKMAIL

Emotional blackmail is a term I have coined to describe a sub-segment of emotional hijacking that has a slightly different operational function. While emotional hijacking can occur in response to just about anything, emotional blackmail almost always involves another person initiating the process. It's usually when influential people in your life use fear, obligation, and guilt to manipulate you. It is a very powerful form of manipulation in which the person directly or indirectly threatens to punish you or withhold a reward if you don't comply with how they want you to behave.

Emotional blackmail is a form of emotional abuse, and it plays on one's emotions and insecurities in an effort to control the victim's behavior and actions. It is often so powerfully subtle that you can be victim of emotional blackmail and not even know it. It may come in the form of a loved one who pouts or gets an attitude, for example.

We are seeing so much of this being brought into the public consciousness today thanks to the #MeToo movement and its efforts to expose the way women have for so long been emotionally blackmailed into being silent about emotional or sexual abuse. They are either directly told or know intuitively that if they tell anyone about their ordeal, their career—their livelihood—will be jeopardized, for example.

Many times we submit to emotional blackmail because we consider the source and decide that it's better to make them happy than not. This causes us to ignore our intuition and, most importantly, our personal truth. Even if we use the threat of emotional blackmail as an excuse for our setbacks, it doesn't change the outcome. It's still a setback. If you stay in a bad relationship, for example, because you are hoping to avoid being emotionally blackmailed by your mate, you are still in a bad relationship and you will still suffer the effects of that bad relationship, perhaps every day of your life.

The way out of emotional hijack and emotional blackmail is awareness. The worst thing that can happen is to be unaware that you are being emotionally manipulated. Now that can send you into emotional hijack. Being emotionally intelligent helps you to put things into perspective and helps to enhance your decision-making in positive ways. Once I understood how my perspective had been altered, either by my own emotions or the emotions of others, I was better able to put things into perspective and ultimately make better decisions. Decision-making involves weighing options and evaluating consequences—two functions that are enhanced by emotional awareness.

EMOTIONAL IMPRISONMENT

Emotional imprisonment is when you consciously decide to stay in a situation, avoid taking action, or hide and allow yourself to be emotionally blackmailed. This puts tight restrictions on your perception of your abilities and will cause you—falsely—to perceive fewer options when making decisions. The result is that you will be trapped into a position of limited opportunities.

Have you noticed how the emotions of others influence your productivity and creativity? Are you ever surrounded by people who make you feel good and productive, or sad and burdened? Have you ever been emotionally connected to someone with limited beliefs or a poverty mindset and noticed that your own creativity, intuition, and positive outlook suffered as a result? Has someone else's emotional drama ever altered your decisions? Have you ever been influenced to do something you didn't really want to do because of the influences of others? If you've had any of these experiences, you likely have been emotionally imprisoned.

I remember a time when I was surrounded by toxic people—people whom I allowed to be very influential in my life and whose emotional agendas were always the prevailing priority. I didn't understand the importance of teaching others how to treat me. I submitted to emotional imprisonment and my intuition and decision-making skills became warped while my productivity suffered. I was so afraid of my emotions and their effect on others that I became emotionally paralyzed and avoided situations when I really should have slowed down and taken a deeper look inside of myself. Now when I am working on making a decision that challenges me emotionally, I spend a significant amount of time strategizing and coming up with other options or smaller steps that will help me to overcome the emotional burden of the decision.

The good news is that it is absolutely possible to break free of emotional imprisonment, no matter how unconscious it has been or familiar it has become. These are the strategies that will help you unlock and walk through the doors that have been limiting your happiness and success:

1. Surround yourself with people who allow you to be emotionally free and with whom you can open up and have fun. Find at least one friend or family member who allows you to express yourself emotionally without judgment. Avoid intimate relationships with people who always have an emotional agenda or who always have to be in control. Seek relationships that offer freedom, balance, and mutual respect.

2. Always take time to check in with yourself. Ask yourself how you are feeling. Sit with any emotions that you feel and allow them to process or pass. Don't be afraid of your own emotions. You will find that when you acknowledge an emotional state, it will

pass faster and more easily than if you ignore it or try to push it away. If you admit to yourself, for example, that you are afraid, you will find that your mind will begin to offer options that help to relieve some of the fear and allow you to analyze if your fear is valid or based on a story that you are telling yourself.

3. Pay attention to your body. Know what "yes" feels like in your body. Become familiar with what love feels like. Learn how to discern when your body is saying "no."

4. Pay close attention and ask questions of those whom you suspect may be trying to manipulate or control you. Ignorance is not bliss.

5. Keep your mind at home. Focus on your own development. Stay out of other folks' business. You have no control over the lives of others. In the words of the Tao Te Ching, "Trust that others know what is best for them."

Emotional intelligence is a fascinating and powerful area of study too involved to cover completely in this book. But understanding the basics can help you to gain awareness and motivate you to study and further your practice in this area.

Studying emotional intelligence is an ongoing process. Your IQ may remain the same but your EQ can always be improved. As a marginalized person working toward becoming an entrepreneur, growing a business, and looking to enjoy groundbreaking success, practicing emotional intelligence is a powerful tool that will help you to overcome obstacles, create success, and enjoy a more fulfilling existence in all areas of your life.

CHAPTER 8

IMPROVE YOUR RELATIONSHIP WITH MONEY

"The letting go of old habitual patterns that have defined a lifetime of dealing with money in a particular way involves an inner realignment and a renewal of energy." — Davide De Angelis

D o you find yourself in a perpetual emotional whirlwind when it comes to money? Does your blood pressure spike when you open a bill? Do you go shopping whenever you're upset or disappointed to make yourself feel better? If you see your neighbor with a new car, do you find yourself wandering aimlessly into a car lot the following weekend? Are you only happy with people who give you things? Do you race to your favorite department store every weekend lusting for the latest designer trends? Do you get a bigger emotional high from spending money than from making it?

Many of us concentrate on the freedom to buy what we want (or on what we can't buy or what we don't have). But the freedom to create what you want is a greater goal. Because if you can create, you can earn.

I am most happy when I am creating. When I am in my creative space, I can almost guarantee success on every level. My most creative efforts have been the most lucrative. This was not always the case: Until I was a young adult, I had a mental disconnection between creating and earning money: I thought I could only pursue my creativity when I wasn't at work. Now I see my business ventures as creative acts.

In April 2018, my business partner, Dr. Jeffery Dormu, and I opened a minimally invasive vascular and weight loss surgery center. The process of creating the concept, developing the real estate, designing the interior, and selecting furniture and light fixtures was one exhilarating moment after another. Standing back and looking at the completed center is one of the most rewarding things in the world to me.

The creative energy we brought to the project attracted an amazing crew who contributed their own passion and commitment. Everyone who visits the center feels the power of creativity. As an entrepreneur I consider myself every bit an artist who gets to create every day. Whether it's designing business systems, choosing art for the walls, or working with architects and engineers, the dynamics of creating help me relieve stress, give me purpose, and keep me excited about life. These emotions set the tone for the rest of my life, including how much money I make. Yes, it's true—when you are able to see yourself as a creator, as opposed to "just" a salesperson or service provider, your income potential explodes.

THE LINK BETWEEN EMOTIONS AND MONEY

Whether you realize it or not, your emotions affect how much money you make and how much money you have. The good news is that when you acknowledge the emotions you have about money and the thoughts that lie underneath them, you can change them. You can raise your money consciousness. And when you do, you can also raise the amount of money that flows to you. It doesn't have to be hard, either: simply shifting your mental focus from spending money to producing money can change the way you think, feel, and act around money.

I know, I know...when you are down on your luck, it's tough to see that the way in which you attract and earn money starts from within. But hear me out. Be open-minded. For any entrepreneur, the concepts in this chapter are extremely important to grasp. Because not only do you want to make more money, you want to keep more money. And if you don't do this work to upgrade your money mindset, it won't matter how much money you make—you'll be like the 30% of lottery winners who end up declaring bankruptcy and find yourself at least as broke or even worse off than when you started.

THE LINK BETWEEN MONEY AND EMOTIONS

Remember, your mind doesn't care whether or not an event is really happening—it only knows what you tell it. So if you are dreaming that you are being chased by a serial killer, your physical body and conscious mind have no idea that you are not really being chased. You may wake up sweating, crying, tired, your heart pounding. It is even possible to have a heart attack in your sleep. Imagine that! But as soon as you wake up and realize it was only a dream, your bodily functions immediately begin to normalize.

In the same way, your brain gets as or even more excited about the thought of making money than it does about actually receiving the check. Conversely, it feels worse when you anticipate not being able to pay your bills than when that actually happens. And since we are thinking about money far more often than we are actually spending or receiving it, those heightened mental states that aren't based on reality tend to be what drive our decisions about money. I have had many people laugh at me when they have heard me talk about money like this. All I can say is, try mentally rehearsing how good it feels to make all the money you need and then some. Just as importantly, redirect your thoughts whenever you notice yourself fretting over bills or income. What else do you have to lose?

Researchers have found that thinking about money taps into the most ancient parts of the brain—the same systems that tell us to run from a tiger. If you never do any work to challenge your thinking about money and to proactively manage your money emotions, you're going to be making financial decisions with all the finesse of a caveman. Even worse, you'll make money decisions like a frightened deer running from a tiger, knowing that it is about to be eaten for dinner.

Now combine these scientific facts with the law of attraction, which tells us that every one of our thoughts, mental images, and feelings draws things to us that match the vibration of those thoughts, images, and feelings. In other words, the things you think and feel create your reality. Think about it; everything you have in your life now you have attracted to you by way of your own mind. So if you are focusing on making money you will create a matching vibration and you will ultimately attract things that match your vibration. Guess what: The same is true if you focus on the fear of losing money.

When I notice myself mentally rehearsing a situation that I do not want, I always ask myself two questions to help me to begin the process of changing my mindset: First I say, "Wendy, what do you want?" And then I ask, "What story are you telling yourself about this situation?"

Now for some of my religious friends out there, I just lost you with my talk of your thoughts creating your reality. Here's a different way to think about: I ask God to make me a vessel and use me to fulfill His purpose. So doesn't it make sense that I clean up my vessel a little bit and take care of it so that I can be used for bigger and greater things? These exercises and mental strategies are just your way of cleaning up and taking care of the vessel that you want God to use. Put yourself in a position so that you can take care of and maintain what you are blessed with.

The simple truth is that your emotions and thoughts affect your decisions and choices. So, if you are consistently emotional about money, you will consistently make decisions about money that are irrational. If you cannot control your emotions, you cannot control your money. If you can't tell your money what to do, it will leave. The most important thing to do is identify the relationship you currently have with money. Once you do that, you can upgrade it. In order to get started, we need to go back to childhood.

DIG UP THE ROOTS OF YOUR MONEY BELIEFS

The events, sayings, and beliefs we're exposed to in childhood affect our grown-up relationship to money. My family was big on slogans and sayings that some consider superstitions. Perhaps your family was too. In our family, the focus was more on spending money, and the only attention paid to creating money was working overtime to get extra money to buy more stuff—cars, diamonds, clothes, houses, etc. One could safely define my parents as ballers. I affectionately refer to them as "original ballers." Because of their influence, I love nice things, and I started my career focused on making money simply so I could buy more nice things. I was forced to learn to think of money differently when I was faced with so much loss in my 20s and early 30s.

I had to change my focus and my values. To change results in life we have to change what we value, what we focus on, and how we see things. To rewrite my money beliefs and establish my own relationship with money, I created new priorities for the money that I earned. The cornerstones of my thoughts about money included a focus on learning; creating and then enjoying the experiences that money makes possible; and protecting the money I made so that I could create more enjoyable experiences in the future. My growing money relationship was also tied to my spiritual development—as I became more confident in knowing that I am here for a reason (as we all are, including you), I saw myself as worthy of money and as being loved by a power greater than me who will make sure I succeed so that I am better equipped to fulfill my purpose.

Just as important to the new thoughts I added to my repertoire about money were the old thoughts I chased out. I now value experiences and creativity. I stopped thinking that there was some mythical figure somewhere who was working to take what I earned and leave me broken and impoverished. I stopped unconsciously believing the sayings that were repeated frequently by my family, including "Money don't grow on trees," "Your friends are them dollars in your pocket," "Stop begging; it makes folks hate you," which were all said with such frequency in my family that I had to uproot them from my own thinking. This family lore had led me to believe that I was worthless if I didn't have any money, and so I had to learn to value myself even if I didn't have it. I also grew up thinking that if I asked someone for help that they would consider me a beggar and hate me. So I had to learn to ask for help if I needed it.

"

Those old thoughts and mindsets worked to get our parents and grandparents to the next level for them. Now, it's our job to create a mindset designed to get us to the next level.

"

Our family members did the best they could with the knowledge and access they had. Now it's time for us to dissect their behavior, deconstruct the thoughts it planted in our own minds, and create new philosophies, experiences, and wealth. Don't spend time bashing your family or parents. You can pick and choose which behaviors you want to model and those that don't serve you today. This doesn't mean you don't love them. You can love someone without imitating their behavior. This may be a point of conflict between you and your family members who have defined love by how much you think and act like them. But your job is to not allow the past to define your future. The past is over and like I always say, the statute of limitations has likely run out on the parent blame game. It's time for you to take responsibility for yourself.

What were you told about money, if anything, from your parents or guardians? If you weren't told or taught anything directly, what was your impression of money growing up? Did you hear things like, "Money don't grow on trees"? Were you afraid of money? Was there always a struggle regarding debt? Were there fights and even violence about money? Did you witness your parents run out and spend every dime they had trying to keep up with the Joneses, so to speak? Or, did your parents scrupulously save every penny and jealously guard their money? Did they pay your way through college with hard-earned money that they worked for and saved all their lives? Did you inherit a large sum of money? Did your parents neglect the conversation altogether and just give you everything you wanted so you now have no concept of money management? Was there a sense of generosity or selfishness? Did your parents spend uncontrollably only to be broke two days after getting paid, and then do it all over again the next payday? Write down whatever those conversations and primary themes were. Yes, I said, "Write it down." Until you get it out of your head and down on paper, you won't be able to have any true objectivity on your relationship to and habitual thoughts and beliefs about money. Awareness is the most important step, because you can't change a habit you don't know you have. Go ahead, I'll wait.

Once you have collected your memories and inherited attitudes about money, take some time to explore how those impressions affect your relationship with money today. Are you a religious saver because your parents were mindless spenders? Do you judge people who have more money than you because that was the way your family talked about family members or total strangers who seemed to be rich? Again, write them down. Again, I'll wait.

Now that you've written down these stories, thoughts, beliefs, and impressions, begin to analyze how they got you where you are today. Even if you're not currently struggling with emotions and money, you can still use this exercise to elevate your money mindset—we all have unhelpful thoughts lurking around the back corners of our minds, many of which can be traced back to something we witnessed and interpreted—or misinterpreted—as truth when we were kids.

Once you identify the thoughts, find ways to transform or recreate them using some of the practical tools that can change your emotional relationship and overall emotions around money. Replace those limited thoughts with those that better align with your goals and what you want. Here are some helpful steps you can take as you work toward building a healthier relationship with money:

1. *Practice gratitude.* Wealth begins with gratitude. When you are in a sincere state of gratitude your energy (your vibe) is one of acceptance and harmony. You resonate at a much higher vi-

brational frequency and you are happier, which is exactly what helps you make choices that connect you to the events, conditions, and circumstances that you desire. To up your gratitude level:

- Keep a gratitude journal or notebook and write down absolutely everything that you're grateful for each night.
- Don't walk past pennies on the sidewalk. Pick them up and be thankful.
- Walk around your house and be grateful for all that you have been able to acquire, no matter how much or how little it is. You created the means to acquire all that you have, certainly you can do it again. This especially works for me when I find myself worried about having enough money or if I buy into the financial gloom and doom on the daily news, for example.
- When you are paying a bill, be grateful. Yes, I said it. Be thankful that you are able to pay it, no matter how hard you had to work to do so. I say thank you and offer a little prayer for every bill I pay.

2. *Focus on production.* Put your mental attention on making money, not spending it. If spending money feels better to you than making money, you've got some work to do. Visualize yourself enjoying the inflow of money. See yourself working on a project that will bring you a sizable income. Hang around people who like making money. What are you producing that can be translated into income? Be creative. Think of something. Your wealth is in your authenticity. Your authenticity is a commodity that no one else owns but you. Give your business your all.

3. *Upgrade your thoughts.* Thoughts either support your creative goals or feed your fears. If you are repeating scenarios in your mind that generate fear around money or your business, then you are sending that vibration right down into your body. Your cells are reacting and your brain is making choices based on the

fear that you manufactured. So, why not manufacture prosperous productive thoughts and react to those?

> " A person's way of doing things is the direct result of the way he thinks about things. To do things in the way you want to do them, you will have to acquire the ability to think the way you want to think. And to think what you want to think is to think truth, regardless of appearances.
> — Wallace Wattles, The Science of Getting Rich "

4. *Harness the power of action.* As important as your thoughts are, once you have them where you want them to be and you've decided what you want, you've got to take a step toward it. Your actions are a logical progression of your thoughts. Don't sit around waiting on an imaginary entity to take care of you. Get up and do something for yourself. Then do the next thing, and the next thing after that. Each action gives you feedback that you can use to refine your thinking and your goals.

5. *Develop your faith.* Visualize that no matter how high gas prices get, for example, you will always have what you need to get what you want. Know that you showed up on the planet with a purpose, and that there will always be a way for you to fulfill your purpose. Why else are you here?

6. *Focus on doing good.* The universe will always reward the doers of good. Build your businesses so that they deliver value to your clients. I call it profiting with a purpose. Focus on solving problems or providing services that help people improve or feel better.

7. *Save, protect, and then spend your money.* Have a healthy amount of money so that you have it when you need it. Save your money, it will save your life. Protect your income and savings so that if you have challenges you can still survive while you figure out how to overcome those challenges. Then know that it is okay to spend money when you use it to do something good. Invest in

yourself as needed. If you need dental work, get it done. If you need a new car, get one. If you need to invest in a gym, do so. It does not create a good feeling to work hard and not have anything to show for it. My father taught me that.

"

Save your money, it will save your life. — Patti Labelle

"

8. *Get up and do something for yourself!* What can you go and do right now to start bringing money toward you? *Go do it!*

AIM FOR OUTSTANDING

"It is proper to welcome struggle. Its arrival is always auspicious. Struggle changes a sub-human into an ideal person. It transforms an ordinary human into a spiritually awake person respected by the world. Struggle is a subtle sculptor who shapes the life of every great spiritual master into a unique and unparalleled work of art." — Swami Kripalu

As technology makes entrepreneurship more accessible (after all, anyone can set up a website and be "open for business" in about an hour) and marginalization forces more people to start their own businesses, today's successful entrepreneurs must be laser-focused on being outstanding in their fields of endeavor. Yesterday, an entrepreneur could settle for just being "good"; today you must be exceptional in order to reap the rewards that a merely okay entrepreneur would have reaped back in the day. Good is no longer acceptable. Outstanding is the new normal. People are looking for extraordinary results and outstanding performances.

The good news is that it is absolutely possible to be outstanding—and stay that way—if you know and follow a few key strategies that are often overlooked by novice entrepreneurs:

"
The problem that people have with problems is that they believe they shouldn't have any. — Tony Robbins
"

1. Accept that you will have problems.

The question isn't whether you will encounter challenges. They are a given. No matter how smart you are, you will encounter problems. The question is, how will you handle the problems that will inevitably come your way? I know how tempting it is to want to hide your problems—it's easy to feel embarrassed by them, or even experience anger and dismay that they have occurred in the first place. But when you look down on yourself and on others who are experiencing difficulties, you restrict your willingness and your ability to think critically and to cope with challenges. Problems can—and must—be seen as opportunities to achieve even greater results.

Growing up I always heard the phase, "Stop begging, it will make folks hate you." So it's no surprise that when I was really struggling and lost everything I owned three times, I felt like I had a contagious disease. It seemed that only other people who were also struggling mightily wanted to be around me. And even they didn't respect me because I was suffering from the same plight they were facing. I spent years trying to overcome that stigma. It wasn't until I didn't give a damn about what other people thought about me that I pulled out of my cycle of struggle and self-doubt. When I was beating myself up for having problems—because if I was so smart, how could I be encountering so much difficulty?—what I didn't realize I was doing was building my identity around the fact that I was struggling. It was only after I saw that I was beating myself up for encountering something that every person who is alive will encounter that I finally started to find a way out of my problems.

Problems are par for the course in life and in business. Not only that, they are excellent teachers and should be welcomed because they give you a chance to prove how powerful you are and to keep refining your critical thinking, problem-solving skills.

2. Focus on the positive.

We've all heard this phrase so much that we pretty much just ignore it. Once I realized I had been letting my problems shape my identity, I knew that I had to find other, more positive ways to view myself. I started to think of myself as a gifted thought leader with extraordinary skills and a supernatural aptitude for business, processes, and strategies. I stopped complaining to my friends and family, because that only perpetuated my focus on what was going wrong. I also stopped posting negative things or anything that alluded to a problem on social media. I was one of the first people to post only uplifting quotes and positive stories on MySpace. My page was filled with positivity. I would get comments like, "This is not what MySpace is for." Or, "This is dumb; you're supposed to tell us about yourself." Nevertheless, I persisted.

When we all navigated to Facebook I only posted positive or problem-solving quotes and lessons from my mentors or from myself. I started a BlogTalkRadio show called The Mind of an Entrepreneur™ and interviewed people on how they overcame problems and challenges in their businesses. I started to change my identity online and it helped me reinvent myself in my real life.

At first, people thought I must be crazy or extremely religious. Now thousands of successful entrepreneurs have built businesses around their positive social media presence. I think I can safely say that I helped to pioneer that manner of using social media. I didn't do it just for myself—I shared content designed to empower and enlighten my followers too. As I studied to become an emotional intelligence coach I created lessons and daily motivation to help others. I would post success stories or lessons from other entrepreneurs. Because I had an entertainment consulting business at the time, I posted stories of success to motivate and guide artists and entertainers coming up in the business. My attitude was, "Let's have some fun with this and put out positive energy so that people can mirror that back to me." It created an upward spiral in my life that helped me re-shape my identity, deliver value to my followers, and develop relationships with potential clients. This re-channeling of my focus changed my life.

3. Hone your coping skills.

Many entrepreneurs are unable to handle problems that arise in their businesses because they simply lack the coping skills and the ability to think critically and objectively analyze options. They are so caught up in their emotions that they engage in a huge cycle of doubt each time they encounter a problem.

I was talking to an entrepreneur recently who was having problems getting an exterior sign installed on her new retail space. It was an older building and they needed to be creative in order to satisfy the regulatory requirements to obtain a sign permit. She was so beside herself with emotion that she told me that she came to me for a strategy on how to get out of her lease and find a new space in a less attractive location with much less visibility.

I asked her, "What are your options regarding the sign?" She answered by ranting about how frustrated she was, how the space wasn't worth it, and how she hated the sign permit office. I asked again, "What are your options?" She continued ranting.

Finally I interrupted her and asked, "What do you really want—do you want to get the exterior sign installed or do you want to walk away from the space?" She kept ranting. I asked her again, "Do you want to get the exterior sign installed or do you want to walk away from the space?" She continued to rant and I walked away and left her standing there. As I did, I could hear her complaining that no one would help her (even though that was exactly what I had been trying to do). I kept going.

The next day I got an email from her thanking me for helping her to figure out what she wanted. She admitted that she had not even weighed her options because she was so upset over the fact that this problem had arisen in the first place. She said she was embarrassed and thought that opening this new store should be going much more smoothly than it was. I replied, "You're welcome. If you are going to be in business you better make problems your best friend." Later I shared with her how I welcome problems and see them as a way to correct my focus and tweak my problem-solving skills. She seemed to think I was amazing for saying that, so I decided to give her some context by telling her the story of the great Madam C.J. Walker.

Madam C.J. Walker was a black woman and the first known American woman to become a self-made millionaire. She was born near Delta, Louisiana, in 1867 as Sarah Breedlove to parents who were recently freed slaves.

At the end of the 19th century—and even today—black women did not consider themselves beautiful because they had been conditioned to believe that anyone with dark skin could never be beautiful. This limited thinking resulted in hopelessness and bottomless self-esteem. In addition, sanitary conditions in rural America, especially among black women, were subpar to say the least. Many black women didn't regularly wash their hair—with indoor plumbing a rarity, particularly in rural areas, they barely had an opportunity to wash their bodies. A good bar of soap was a luxury, let alone shampoo. Many slept in unsanitary conditions and suffered from lice, dandruff, and scalp disease. Moreover, they struggled to earn a living for themselves outside of voluntary or involuntary servitude—mostly to white families who often mistreated or even abused them long after slavery was abolished.

When in her 20s, Madam C.J. Walker's own hair began to fall out in clumps on her pillow at night. She attended a seminar where she learned a formula designed specifically for black hair. Then she began manufacturing and packaging this product and teaching a lifestyle of hygiene to black women. Walker also created a sales and distribution process that empowered other black women to become saleswomen and entrepreneurs by giving them a product to sell that solved a problem.

When black women saw Madam C.J. Walker and her team with healthy, clean, and styled hair, they began to feel that they too could be beautiful. Madam C.J. Walker traveled throughout the United States and the Caribbean selling her products and empowering black women to become beauty entrepreneurs. This was at a time when black women could not vote, were unable to enter many establishments, and lacked education. She purchased and drove a car, owned property (including a townhouse in Harlem in New York City), supported the NAACP, provided scholarships, and built homes and factories.

How many problems do you think Madam C.J. Walker encountered in her quest to develop and grow her business? How much pushback do you imagine she experienced? How do you think people reacted to seeing her driving a car? There is even a famous photo of her driving her car with all women passengers, one of which is a white woman (or a very light skinned black woman) who sat in the backseat! How about depositing money in the bank, building a home, building a factory, and hiring and managing employees? And you think you have problems? Do you think she had a temper tantrum and threatened to quit every time she had a problem, or do you think she found solutions?

If Madam C.J. Walker could create such phenomenal success despite almost incomprehensively overwhelming odds, you can get better at coping. All the strategies I've outlined in this book will help you do just that.

4. Take care of your body.

Although this book is designed to help you develop the mental sharpness and resilience to think like an entrepreneur, your physical body is an essential piece of the equation. As a whole person there is no separation between your mind and your body. Your professional intuition may speak to you via a feeling in your stomach, a heaviness in your chest, or even a case of goose bumps when you meet someone who will be important to your success.

As we covered in Chapter 3, your thoughts form your beliefs. And your beliefs dictate the way you see the world. Together, your thoughts and beliefs also create your energy—if you are thinking negative thoughts, or listening to and believing the doom-and-gloom headlines we're bombarded with every day, your energy will vibrate at a lower frequency. Your frequency affects everything, including your biology. In this way, poor emotional health can weaken your body's immune system, making you more likely to get colds and other infections during emotionally difficult times, for example.

It was when I was a college student that I first discovered the connection between my emotions and my health. Under pressure to do well in class, I had developed near-constant stomach aches and acid reflux. I finally figured out that if I worried, I got sick, but if I focused on solutions, I felt good, I was successful and vibrant, and I actually stayed healthy.

I am by no means the only person who advocates for tending to the mind via taking care of the body. Both the Canadian Mental Health Association and the UK-based Mental Health Foundation put physical exercise/activity as the first key solution for improving mental well-being. A study in the Primary Care Companion to the Journal of Clinical Psychiatry states that "Exercise improves mental health by reducing anxiety, depression, and negative mood and by improving self-esteem and cognitive function. Exercise has also been found to alleviate symptoms such as low self-esteem and social withdrawal."

I cite this quote because you can't afford any of these problems if you are going to develop the mind of an entrepreneur and be highly successful. To the contrary, you need to be able to function at the highest cognitive and intellectually creative levels to grow and problem solve your business ventures and to exceed expectations for your clients and customers. Moreover, you will never succeed if you have low self-esteem or experience chronic depression and tend to withdraw socially. Rather, you need to be boldly confident and approachable, and the exhilaration that springs from exercise can help you do all these things.

An entrepreneur who is in poor health is less likely to be extraordinarily successful. Simply put, your business can only be as healthy as you are, particularly in the beginning phases when your business is most likely to consist only of you and requires most of your mental and physical energy.

> "
> **Your business can only be as healthy as you are, particularly in the beginning phases when your business is most likely to consist only of you.**
> "

Because there is no whistle that blows at the end of the day, as an entrepreneur it is tempting to adopt the habits of workaholism—sitting for 10 to 12 hours a day, existing in a state of constant low-grade stress that you never take steps to mitigate, skipping meals only to binge later on something unhealthy simply because it's easy to grab and eat at your desk. But your longevity and your business's longevity will both be severely impaired if you don't take care of your body.

According to the Mental Health Foundation, "even a short burst of 10 minutes brisk walking increases our mental alertness, energy and positive mood." Everyone can find 10 minutes. Especially once you realize that by stepping away from your work and doing something nice for your body you are nearly always rewarded with a flash of insight or a new perspective that makes the rest of your efforts more productive.

I myself neglected my physical health until about five years ago, even though I knew better. After all, I grew up watching my parents work out. My mom taught aerobics and played in softball and volleyball leagues my entire childhood. My dad regularly played basketball and racquetball. Our lives revolved around sporting events and physical activity. I had known for a long time how important it was to keep one's body in shape, but it took me longer to connect the dots between physical fitness and entrepreneurial success.

I went through a series of exercise programs—including hiking, kickboxing, and hot yoga—before I discovered CrossFit and Alpha Fitness. Again and again, these activities that I took on in the name of physical fitness have helped me work through emotional blind spots that could have been silently hindering my personal success. I've left lots of anger, fear, and sadness on the gym floor. And pushing myself to do workouts that I either didn't want to do or would not normally do has created a lot of mental flexibility and toughness that has raised my awareness of what I am capable of. Challenging your body in different ways can help to create breakthroughs in all aspects of your life.

Working out and focusing on my mental and physical health has helped me discover when I have been sitting on a plateau without pushing myself to the next level—what I view as a form of functional depression. Getting back to the gym (or yoga studio, or dance class) always makes me feel more courageous and open to challenges. Just as you are taking ownership of your business, you must take ownership of your health.

There is no one exercise or health prescription that fits all. Whatever works for your body is what you must do. Beyond exercise, I also study how my body responds to certain foods. Once I determine that a category of food doesn't suit my physiology, I take care to avoid it, and don't worry if people think I'm picky with my food choices. I also study how my body reacts to certain environments and design my home and office to support what enables me to be in peak performance and in the right emotional state. I take responsibility for the energy I bring to the office, to every conversation, and to negotiations. You must be the master of your mind and your body.

I recently heard one of my virtual mentors, Tony Robbins (whom I have been studying for over 25 years now) say, and I'm paraphrasing, "I don't negotiate with my own mind. I tell my mind what to do and I say 'motherfucker you do it.'" That was one of the most powerful things I have ever heard him say and he says a lot of great stuff! It resonated with me because I can't tell you how many times I have found myself negotiating with my own mind when it says, "I'm tired, I'm done, I'm sick, I don't feel like it." Building your strength and your stamina through an exercise program will help you tell your mind to fall in line and help you do what you know must be done in order to be happy and successful.

YOU HAVE SOMETHING TO CONTRIBUTE

Today's markets reward nothing less than utter authenticity, extraordinary performance, and outstanding contribution. In order to deliver these qualities, you must be able to achieve and maintain peak performance. You must remain pliable during transformation. And to do so, you need the mental and physical stamina of an athlete. The more marginalized you are, the more focused and resilient you need to be. I know you are probably wondering if you can do it, but I'm here to say that not only can you do it but you likely have no choice.

You must get up and do something for yourself. You have to figure it out. Pound the pavement, go door to door, and sell your services. Open your mouth. Closed mouths don't get fed.

I was giving an entrepreneurial pep talk to someone once and they said, "Wendy, starting a business takes a miracle." Well, you are already a miracle. Why would a Creator who so masterfully designed your physical body with a heart that beats over 100,000 times per day, 206 bones that work in concert with each other, enough blood vessels to stretch over 100,000 miles, and a sophisticated brain with over 100 billion nerve cells leave you limited to only what someone else can give you and only if you behave the way they want you to behave? You can always contribute more, you can always care more, and you can always earn more. If you are looking to someone else to create your livelihood, or talking yourself out of your desires to make a bigger contribution and reap bigger rewards, you are limiting yourself. And why would you want to limit a miracle?

CPSIA information can be obtained
at www.ICGtesting.com
Printed in the USA
LVHW030221230320
650882LV00002B/759